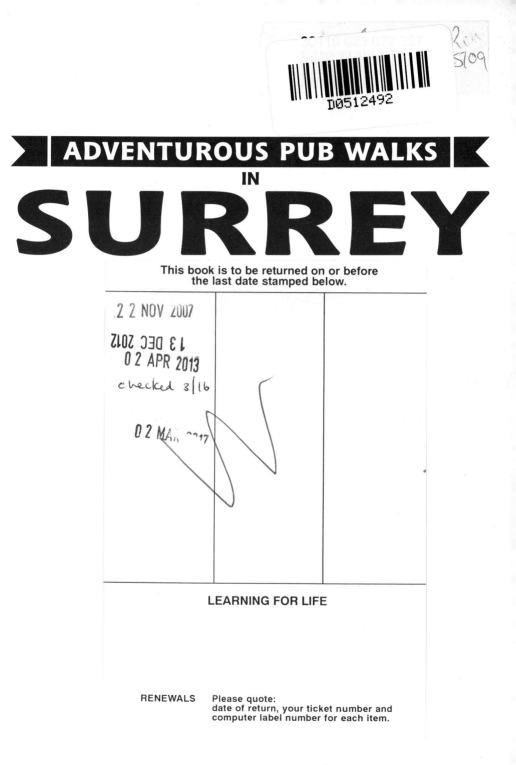

# ADVENTUROUS PUB WALKS
## IN
# SURREY

This book is to be returned on or before
the last date stamped below.

2 2 NOV 2007

13 DEC 2012

0 2 APR 2013

checked 3/16

0 2 MAR 2017

LEARNING FOR LIFE

First published 2004
© David Weller 2004

COUNTRYSIDE BOOKS
3 Catherine Road
Newbury, Berkshire

To view our complete range of books,
please visit us at
www.countrysidebooks.co.uk

ISBN 1 85306 832 2

Designed by Peter Davies, Nautilus Design
Maps and photographs by the author

Cover picture of Hackhurst Downs, from Abinger Roughs,
supplied by Derek Forss

Produced through MRM Associates Ltd., Reading
Typeset by Techniset Typesetters, Newton-le-Willows
Printed by Woolnough Bookbinding Ltd., Irthlingborough

# CONTENTS

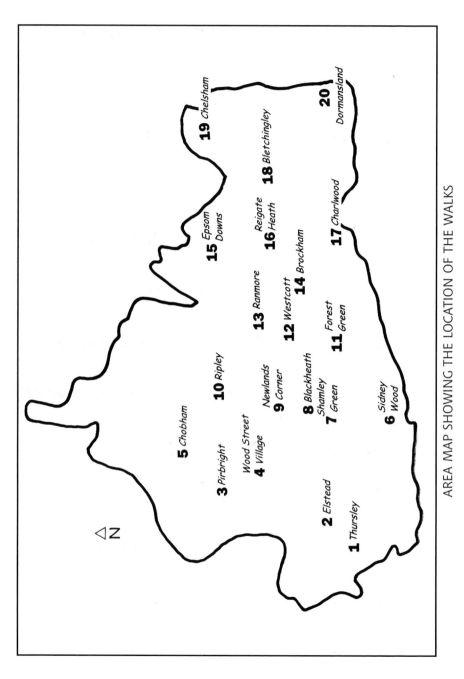

N △

1 Thursley
2 Elstead
3 Pirbright
4 Wood Street Village
5 Chobham
6 Sidney Wood
7 Shamley Green
8 Blackheath
9 Newlands Corner
10 Ripley
11 Forest Green
12 Westcott
13 Ranmore
14 Brockham
15 Epsom Downs
16 Reigate Heath
17 Charlwood
18 Bletchingley
19 Chelsham
20 Dormansland

AREA MAP SHOWING THE LOCATION OF THE WALKS

# INTRODUCTION

I was so thrilled to be asked to write this, my sixth walking book, with a brief to find some unusual longer routes – 7 to 13 miles or so – each providing a good day's ramble. My previous books have been collections of shorter circuits and I was beginning to wonder if I was capable of walking further. So, not exactly in the bloom of youth and rather overweight, I was about to find out. My dog Emma always accompanies me on my travels through the Surrey countryside and she is also not as young as she would like, so for both of us it was a great, not to be missed challenge. Well, having walked, photographed, written and, above all, thoroughly enjoyed these routes, we are living proof that you need not be a finely-honed athlete to complete even the longest of them. They are all circular, easy to follow and none too strenuous and, as far as feasible, I have avoided as many hills as I could but, with a total distance of around 200 miles, it is impossible not to have some ups and downs.

With the sun on your back and great views over the Surrey countryside ahead, the miles just melt away and there is nothing to beat the experience. The routes lead you easily through the best scenery the county can provide: appealing villages where rose-adorned cottages line a pretty village green, scenic fields with breathtaking views, the shimmering waters of rivers, streams and brooks, and glorious shaded woodland with proud old trees. Some routes follow parts of the ancient Pilgrims' Way, more latterly adopted as the North Downs Way, while others take in parts of the Greensand Way, the Downs Link, the Vanguard Way and the Wey South Path, all long-distance footpaths that crisscross the county.

It is always good to walk during spring and summer when myriads of wildflowers are blooming and wildlife abounds, but to wander through woodland during autumn, discovering clusters of toadstools and mushrooms displaying themselves under trees bathed in glorious golds and browns, is not to be missed. Even the dead of winter brings its own joys as you crunch over frosted ground and discover new vistas that have opened up through the leafless trees.

I have featured pubs on each route that offer a warm welcome to walkers passing the door and give good value. Where better to take a break along the way than in a sunny pub garden with ample supplies of wholesome food and liquid refreshment? During winter many of the pubs have glowing log fires that exude bags of atmosphere and warm you through and through, although I would ask that you take your muddy boots off before entering. Where appropriate I have mentioned other establishments that also offer refreshment along some routes.

The best piece of advice I can give regarding these splendid walks is to start with the shorter ones first and to pace yourself. Remember, it is not a race and the longer you take the more you will see, as along the way you will pass ancient buildings that require more than just a glance and there is always plenty to catch the eye in the hedgerows, fields and woods. As a rough guide, allow around $2^1/_2$ miles per hour – and please always obey the Country Code.

As for the equipment required, I would recommend stout walking boots and long trousers as I have seen too many people in shorts trying to negotiate nettles and brambles to recommend anything else. My maps are drawn to scale but it is desirable to also bring along an Ordnance Survey map so that you can gain a better oversight of the circuit. Maps 186 and 187 of the Landranger series cover all of these walks.

I am sure you will get as much enjoyment from these great walks as I did in creating them.

David Weller

## ACKNOWLEDGEMENTS

*I am indebted to Marilyn, my long suffering wife, who not only cheerfully accompanies me on some of my published walks, but also has the diligence to proof-read my manuscripts and the patience to put up with my rattling on about new routes and projects that I am planning.*

## PUBLISHER'S NOTE

*W*e hope that you obtain considerable enjoyment from this book; great care has been taken in its preparation. Although at the time of publication all routes followed public rights of way or permitted paths, diversion orders can be made and permissions withdrawn.

We cannot, of course, be held responsible for such diversion orders and any inaccuracies in the text which result from these or any other changes to the routes nor any damage which might result from walkers trespassing on private property. We are anxious though that all details covering the walks are kept up to date and would therefore welcome information from readers which would be relevant to future editions.

The simple sketch maps that accompany the walks in this book are based on notes made by the author whilst checking out the routes on the ground. However, for the benefit of a proper map, we do recommend that you purchase the relevant Ordnance Survey sheet covering your walk. The Ordnance Survey maps are widely available, especially through booksellers and local newsagents.

# THURSLEY, THE DEVIL'S PUNCH BOWL AND BOWLHEAD GREEN

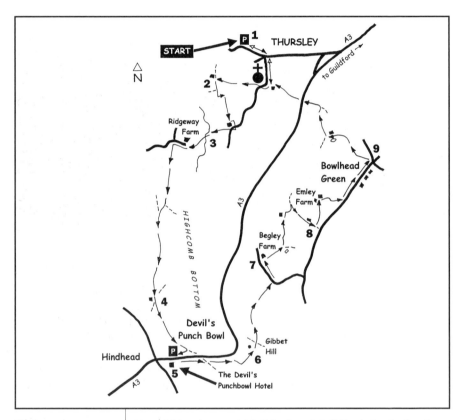

**Distance:**
8 miles

**Starting point:**
Thursley cricket
pitch. GR: 900398

Map: OS Landranger 186 Aldershot & Guildford, Camberley &
Haslemere

**How to get there:** *Thursley is 3 miles south-west of
Milford and 1/2 mile from the A3. A grassy parking area
will be found next to the village cricket pitch at the western
end of the village.*

THE MAGNIFICENT VIEW FROM GIBBET HILL

*T*his glorious circuit has everything – centuries old farmhouses, wide tracks, superb woodland, fantastic views and even a murder mystery. The walk begins in Thursley and soon passes its old church before continuing along easily followed field paths. Soon after traversing a charming woodland dell and crossing a clear running stream, the way begins a steady climb on a wide track through pine woodland to reach the Devil's Punch Bowl, one of Surrey's best-loved beauty spots.

As you leave this popular place behind you soon meet up with the lesser-known Gibbet Hill where the views are stunning. The path now descends through woodland before crossing pretty fields and continuing through an idyllic vale to reach and pass by lovely Emley Farmhouse. Before long, the way continues past the old houses of pretty Bowlhead Green before returning to Thursley on easily followed paths to meet the end of this excellent walk.

William Cobbett once described Hindhead as 'the most villainous spot that God ever made'. As a farmer he was actually referring to the poor greensand soil that made farming impossible. The only people who could scratch some sort of a living here were a few 'broom squires' who lived in Highcomb Bottom and they only made ends meet by a spot of poaching. During the 18th century the area's popularity increased, necessitating the building of the **Devil's Punchbowl Hotel**. Formally a temperance hotel, it has much changed – as the beers testify. From the pumps come Tetley's Smooth, Bass and Wadworth 6X plus Guinness, Stella Artois and Carlsberg lagers and Dry Blackthorn cider. There is an excellent range of food from simple snacks like filled jacket potatoes to Buccleuch T-bone steaks with all the trimmings. Vegetarians also have a good choice from both the snack and the main menu.

**Opening times** *are from 11 am to 11 pm (Sunday 12 noon to 10.30 pm). For non-alcoholic beverages the hotel opens from 7 am on weekdays and 8 am at weekends. Cooked food can be ordered between 12 noon and 3 pm and 6 pm to 10 pm (Sunday 12 noon to 9 pm). Booking is essential. Telephone: 01428 606565.*

# The Walk

① From the cricket pitch, walk alongside the road in the direction of the A3 and soon turn right along a road called **The Street**. Follow the road to meet **St Michael's church** and go right over a stile to enter the graveyard. Continue beside the church to meet a directional post where our way continues alongside a wall. Near this post is the tombstone of an unknown sailor whose murder is roughly depicted above a sad epitaph that can still be deciphered; two of the lines read:

*In perfect health and in the flower of age
I fell victim to three ruffians' rage.*

**In the September of 1786, an unknown sailor making his way to Portsmouth was befriended by three other sailors returning to their ships. After spending the evening in the Red Lion at Thursley, they all continued on their way together. The next day a shepherd, who had also been in the Red Lion that fateful night, discovered the unknown sailor's naked body at the Devil's Punch Bowl. The three men were caught**

*selling his clothes, identified, arrested and hung for their crime. The Red Lion is now a private residence.*

Press on along the left side of the churchyard where we join a section of the **Greensand Way** long distance path. Exit via a kissing gate and continue ahead on a fenced path to meet a field. Cross the field towards a house to meet a lane. (*³/₄ mile*)

② Turn left along the lane and at a sharp right bend, continue ahead on a footpath signposted **GW**. The path soon bends to the left and continues between fields to reach a stile. Cross this and now go along the right-hand field edge where you follow the **GW** arrows. After skirting a large garden the path ends at a road. Turn right along the road and in 30 yards, at a left bend, leave the **Greensand Way** by pressing on ahead over a stile and continuing on

RUSSELL'S BAR AT THE DEVIL'S PUNCHBOWL HOTEL HAS THE ATMOSPHERE OF A GOOD VILLAGE LOCAL

a narrow fenced path. After crossing a second stile, the path descends quite steeply into a woodland dell and meets a stream. (³/₄ mile)

**The Greensand Way long distance path was created in 1980 and its 55-mile length stretches from Haslemere to the Kent border near Westerham.**

③ Go ahead over a wooden bridge and continue up a fairly steep and eroded path. After levelling, the path passes **Ridgeway Farm**, which has parts dating from the early 15th century. Keep ahead now along a tarmac lane to meet a small road junction in a dip. Turn left here on a rising bridleway between banks.

As you exit this almost subterranean world you pass by a National Trust sign and meet a gate. Press on through the gate and remain on the broad track. At the top of a rise by a marker post, ignore paths to left and right and keep ahead with power cables to your right. Later, at another junction of tracks by a marker post, keep ahead and eventually go under a height barrier. In 30 yards, when beside a radio mast, fork left. (³/₄ mile)

④ Now ignore any side paths and continue ahead to eventually meet open hillside on your left and wide steps to your right. Turn right up these steps and continue through the National Trust car park to meet the **Devil's Punchbowl Hotel**. The National Trust café here is open each day during daylight hours. (1¹/₄ miles)

⑤ After taking well-earned refreshment, continue along a wide track that begins opposite the exit of the National Trust car park. (Make sure that you follow the track that remains parallel to the A3.) Soon ignore a crossing track and keep ahead.

At a fork by a marker post go straight on along the main track, but soon turn right by a sign directing you to **Gibbet Hill**. In 25 yards pass to the left of a National Trust sign to reach the open hillside some 880 feet above sea level with far-reaching views. (¹/₂ mile)

**After the three perpetrators of the sailor's murder had been tried and executed, their bodies were hung in chains from gibbets on this open hillside and it was not until three years later that their bones fell to the ground during a violent storm. The once pretty name of Butterwedge Hill has since become known for all time as Gibbet Hill.**

⑥ The way is leftwards where you should seek out a narrow path 10 yards to the right of a tall memorial stone marking the site of the gibbet. The path leads you through trees where in 60 yards you should go ahead over a crossing track by a marker post. As you descend, keep ahead at a second and a third marker post. The narrow path begins to level and passes between silver birch trees before descending more steeply between banks and stands of pine. The path ends beside the entranceway to **Boundless Farm** where you should now turn left along a lane. *(³/₄ mile)*

⑦ At the entranceway to **Begley** Farm, turn right through a kissing gate. Continue over a field to a second kissing gate and press on along a line of trees. Some 35 yards after passing the remains of an old swimming pool, the path divides and you should turn left here and cross a stile beside a field gate.

Now go right along the field edge to meet and cross a stile at the far end. Pass through a strip of woodland to enter a small field by a house. Go diagonally right and pass the house to reach a stile at the far side. Go over the stile and turn right along a drive and keep to it when it soon turns sharply right. As you look

**EMLEY FARMHOUSE, PASSED ON THE ROUTE**

back over this captivating scene, you must wonder if there could ever be a prettier place to live. (³/₄ mile)

⑧ After passing a couple of houses, the drive continues between fields where you meet a stile on your left. Cross this and continue up a rising field to a stile in the edge of woodland. Press on ahead on a short, but steep path between the trees to meet the crest of the hill. Go over a stile at the far side and descend down the left edge of a field to meet the wonderful buildings of **Emley Farm**.

*The farmhouse is mid 16th century and is one of the best-preserved examples of its type in Surrey. The barns are from the 17th and 18th centuries. Thankfully the National Trust has saved the farm for the nation.*

Turn right by the farmhouse and continue along the drive until it meets a road. Turn left along the

road and pass the superb houses and farm in **Bowlhead Green**. (³/₄ mile)

⑨ At a crossroads by the village green our way turns sharply left on a signposted bridleway. Follow the bridleway until it finally meets a track where we bear left and pass between an ornamental pond and a house.

At a driveway by the entrance to **Cosford Farm**, go ahead and soon, at a fork, continue rightwards along the drive. When the drive meets another by electronic gates, turn left along the drive and soon ignore a path on your right. Keep ahead to meet and cross the busy A3 dual carriageway where the route continues on a path opposite. At a field, go diagonally right towards a house to meet a rough track. Here go rightwards along it to soon rejoin **The Street** where you should turn right and retrace your steps to the start of this scenic walk. (1³/₄ miles)

*Date walk completed:*

# ELSTEAD, FRENSHAM LITTLE POND AND RUSHMOOR

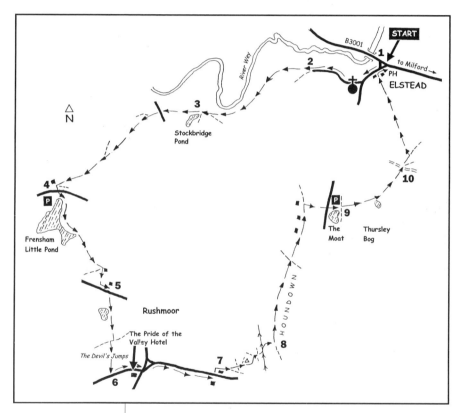

**Distance:**
10¹/₂ miles

**Starting point:**
Elstead village green. GR: 907437

Map: OS Landranger 186 Aldershot & Guildford, Camberley & Haslemere

**How to get there:** *Elstead is 2 miles west of the A3 at Milford and is on the B3001. Park beside the small triangular village green or in a layby along Thursley Road.*

THE PRIDE OF THE VALLEY HOTEL IS TUCKED AWAY IN THE TREES AT RUSHMOOR AND IS A SUPER WATERING HOLE

*T*his great circuit begins in the ancient wool centre of Elstead. The route is easy to follow and attractive, and has a watery theme as the way passes several heathland pools, the largest of which is Frensham Little Pond. From here the path passes another pretty pond before continuing between the strange conical hills known as The Devil's Jumps to reach the Pride of the Valley Hotel at Rushmoor and good refreshment.

Leaving Rushmoor behind, the route continues east where it crosses a part of Hankley Common to meet a wonderful track at Houndown, a wooded backwater. After following the track for some way, the direction turns to meet The Moat, another heathland pool and a haven for wildlife. Continuing over Elstead Common and passing Thursley Bog, an important Site of Special Scientific Interest (SSSI), the terrain soon changes from sandy heath to the lush green fields of Pot Common where an attractive path brings you back to Elstead.

Nestling in a pretty little valley amongst the trees and not far from the mythical Devil's Jumps is the **Pride of the Valley Hotel**. The Victorian built establishment was once Prime Minister David Lloyd George's local and he is remembered in the signage outside. Since a serious fire in 1998 that forced the hotel's temporary closure, an imaginative refurbishment programme has taken place for the benefit of all. The oak panelled restaurant is comfortable and boasts a superb selection of dishes that include honey glazed sea bass with rosti potatoes and squid-ink sauce. Lighter bites can be obtained in the bar, which has unusual furnishings on a Welsh dragon theme, whilst from the pumps comes a guest beer that changes weekly as well as well-kept Fuller's London Pride and Gale's HSB.

*Opening times are from 11 am to 11 pm (Sunday 12 noon to 10.30 pm), with cooked food available from 12 noon to 3 pm and 7 pm to 10 pm (Sunday 12 noon to 3 pm only). Booking for the popular restaurant is essential. Telephone: 01428 695799.*

 *The Walk*

① Leave the village green by walking along **Thursley Road**, signposted to **Thursley** and **Churt**, and turn right into **Westbrook Hill** by **St James' church**. Follow this lane and after passing the fenced grounds of **Westbrook House** on your left you will meet a junction of tracks by a gateway. (*3/4 mile*)

② Bear right here on a bridleway along a track and very soon, at a fork beside an MoD sign, leave the track by forking right on a narrower path through trees. Keep ahead at a crossing path and soon remain parallel to a field on your right. Press on over a track and before

long the way is met by a wider track. Continue ahead and, at a junction of paths beside a tennis court, go straight on along the signed bridleway. In 80 yards keep right at a fork and now ignore all side paths until you meet a junction of tracks in a clearing. Keep ahead here on the bridleway which descends between shallow banks to meet another MoD sign by a vehicle barrier. (*1 mile*)

③ Go ahead and pass **Stockbridge Pond** on a wide track that ends at a road. Cross to a track opposite and in 120 yards fork left. Now remain on this track until it finally reaches a junction of paths besides public conveniences. Ignore a sharp left turn here but turn left on a grassy path that soon brings you to a road

beside **Frensham Little Pond**.
*(1¹/₂ miles)*

④ Bear left along the water's edge and cross a small wooden bridge. Continue rightwards around the edge of the pond on a well-worn path and when this begins to leave the pond, keep left at a fork. At a barrier by a National Trust sign, go ahead on a fenced path. Ignore a left fork by a field gate and continue ahead to reach a second barrier where you should maintain direction. In 40 yards ignore a

bridleway to left and right, but in a further 10 yards, turn right on a bridleway that passes the side of gardens to meet a road.
*(1¹/₄ miles)*

⑤ Go left along the road and when opposite the drive to a house named **Middlestone**, turn right on a bridleway. As the bridleway leads you towards **The Devil's Jumps**, it passes another pretty heathland pool. Keep ahead until the bridleway ends at a junction of tracks. Here go right for 5 yards

**SEATS DOTTED ALONG THE BANKS OF FRENSHAM LITTLE POND ENCOURAGE YOU TO STAY AWHILE AND ADMIRE THE VIEW**

before turning left and maintaining your original direction on a wide path that initially passes to the left of a field. The path rises slowly and passes between two of the knolls that form **The Devil's Jumps** and finally reaches a road. *(1 mile)*

*The three conical hills that make up The Devil's Jumps have been associated with the Devil since Saxon times. According to legend, the Devil with horns gleaming and tail flying would amuse himself by jumping from one hilltop to another. Thor, the Saxon god, caught him playing his foolish game and bowled him over with an enormous stone that remains on top of one of the hills to this day.*

⑥ Turn left along the road to meet the **Pride of the Valley Hotel** where well-earned sustenance can be obtained. From the hotel, press on a few yards further to a road junction and continue along the road signposted to **Thursley** and **Elstead**. When the entranceway to **Stream Cottage** is met, you should go left on a track and pass a vehicle barrier by an MoD sign. *(1 mile)*

⑦ Turn right here along a wide track where you pass the rear of a garden. Keep to the track as it rises and, 80 yards after passing over the crest of the rise, fork leftwards. In 50 yards, keep ahead over a

crossing track to meet a junction of paths in 80 yards. Keep ahead here on a rising path and ignore a left fork when near the top of the rise. Within yards you will find yourself beside a rather eroded trig point where the views are quite outstanding. Pass the trig point and bear left on an eroded downhill path and when a track joins it from the left, bear right along it to soon meet a large junction of tracks. Keep ahead here on a stony bridleway and when the bridleway broadens and is met by another, keep ahead. In 130 yards, at a wide junction of tracks, bear right to meet a crossing track in 30 yards. Now turn right along this crossing track and continue downhill to pass under power cables at the bottom of the slope. Continue left here along the line of cables and when you reach the first pylon, turn right on a wide sandy track that at first rises before descending to meet a T-junction with a hard surfaced bridleway. *($^1/_2$ mile)*

⑧ Turn left now and stay on this bridleway as it leads you through woodland. When a road cuts across the way, press on ahead and pass a few secluded houses. When opposite the gates to **Elstead Manor**, you should turn right along a track that brings you to a road. Cross the road and go right through a parking area to meet the bank of **The Moat**. *($1^1/_2$ miles)*

⑨ Continue leftwards along the bank and in 50 yards, at a crossing track, press on ahead. Pass under power cables by an MoD sign and maintain direction along a wide bridleway. The sharper eyed of you will see the tiny sundew, Britain's only insectivorous plant, growing along here in summer. **Thursley Bog** lies to your right; so make sure you keep to the bridleway. Later the track narrows and passes through woodland to reach a wide crossing track. *(3/4 mile)*

*Thursley Bog cannot be reached from this bridleway but is worth a separate visit. The bog can be visited via the southern end of The Moat, where there is a path that leads to the bog. English Nature has provided boarded walkways so that the more inaccessible parts may by viewed.*

*The bog is ecologically important and contains many rare plants, insects and birds.*

⑩ Go over the crossing track to meet a bridleway that immediately forks. Keep left here and soon it passes close by a field, at the end of which you should cross a stile on your left. Now follow the left side of a couple of fields to meet a cart track. Press on along the track and at a third field keep ahead along the left side to reach another cart track. At a junction of tracks, go ahead over a stile and maintain direction along the right-hand side of a field. At the far side continue on a downhill fenced path that brings you to **Thursley Road**. Turn right here to soon reach **Elstead's** green and the end of this superb walk. *(1 1/4 miles)*

Date walk completed:

# PIRBRIGHT, FOX CORNER AND NORMANDY

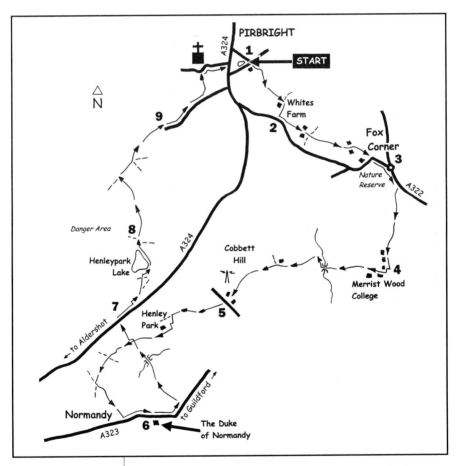

**Distance:**
9¹/₂ miles

**Starting point:**
Pirbright village green. GR: 946559

**Map:** OS Landranger 186 Aldershot & Guildford, Camberley & Haslemere

**How to get there:** *Pirbright is on the A324 and 4¹/₂ miles north-west of Guildford. Park alongside the village green near the Cricketers pub.*

THE WALK STARTS BY PIRBRIGHT'S PICTURESQUE VILLAGE DUCK POND

*T*his enjoyable circuit begins at Pirbright's large well-kept green and glorious duck pond. After crossing pretty meadows and going through oak woodland, the route reaches Fox Corner, a small hamlet blessed with a large area set aside for wildlife. The way turns south here and continues past Merrist Wood, a house designed in 1877 by Norman Shaw and now finding new life as an agricultural college. From here the route turns and follows a low ridge through woodland as it heads for 18th century Henley Park, another fine old Surrey house now finding new use.

Dropping down the ridge brings the circuit to the Duke of Normandy pub on the edge of Normandy village. The path now heads back over pretty meadows and rejoins Henley Park, where it continues on to reach the scenic waters of Henleypark Lake. After following the water's edge for a while, the route continues along easy paths and wide tracks through majestic woodland to rejoin the green at Pirbright.

Apart from being the place where William Cobbett, the 19th century writer and thorny commentator on Surrey, lived, Normandy has added little to history. He died at Normandy Farm during the summer of 1835 and one must wonder what he would have said about the transfer here in 1870 of Guildford's horse races. They became so lawless that large mobs of people roamed the area robbing all in their way. I am glad to say things have changed greatly for the better nowadays and you will find that passing through here is much more pleasurable, especially when you visit the **Duke of Normandy** pub.

The pub garden makes a good spot to relax and enjoy Greene King's IPA and the stronger Abbot Ale while you consume a hearty meal from the menu that includes a honey roast ham dish. Look out for the house specials on the blackboard, as these are always good value. For a lighter snack there are plenty of jacket potato, flat bread and baguette choices.

**Opening times** *at lunchtime are from 11.30 am to 3 pm on Monday to Saturday and 12 noon to 3 pm on Sunday. Evening opening is from 5.30 pm to 11 pm on weekdays, 6 pm to 11 pm on Saturday and 7 pm to 10.30 pm on Sunday. Cooked food is served during each session except Sunday evening. Booking is advisable for meals. Telephone: 01483 235157.*

## The Walk

① Go along a drive to the left of the **Cricketers** pub, signed as a public footpath, and fork left into a plant nursery by the gates of a cottage named **Tarrens**. Soon turn right on a signposted path that leads you past the end of greenhouses. Press on ahead through woodland on a path that leads you to a stile at a field edge. Cross the stile and continue diagonally right to a second stile before turning left to meet the driveway of **Whites Farm**. Continue rightwards along the drive until it ends at a road. (*3/4 mile*)

② Turn left along a redundant piece of road and fork left by a field gate on an enclosed path. Press on ahead at a driveway to reach a junction of paths. Maintain direction ahead on a path through oak woodland to reach a house where the way forks left along a tarmac drive and passes **Heath Mill** and its dilapidated waterwheel. Keep to this little lane until it ends at a road in **Fox Corner** where the **Fox** pub is a few yards on your right if you are in need of refreshment. (*1 mile*)

③ The way is ahead along the larger road where you will soon pass by a wonderful nature reserve to reach a roundabout.

*It is hard to believe that not long ago this area was an eyesore and used for illegal dumping. After it had been compulsorily purchased by Guildford Borough Council in 1989, the local residents petitioned for the creation of a wildlife area. This was granted in 1990 and they formed their own charity to run this lovely place on a 50-year lease.*

Bear right along **Worplesdon Road** and, 80 yards after passing a bakery, go right over a stile to enter the grounds of **Merrist Wood**

**College**. Go diagonally left over a field to reach and cross a stile. Now bear left along a hedgerow and cross a stile at the top of a rise. Keep ahead along the well-signed path to reach a concrete drive. Pass various buildings to reach a T-junction by a car park. *(1 mile)*

④ Turn right here and, in a few yards, go left between classrooms to reach a road. Turn right alongside the road to reach the college's main reception. Maintain direction ahead over a grassy area with **Merrist**

THE DUKE OF NORMANDY PUB SITS AT THE EASTERN END OF THE VILLAGE

**Wood** house to your left. Ignore a stile ahead of you and seek out a path 15 yards to its right. After following the edge of woodland, cross a stile ahead of you and continue ahead along a cart track between fields to reach a bridge over a stream. Turn right here and, at the end of a field on your left, turn left on a path that skirts a golf course. At a clearing, continue ahead to the top left corner and press on along a narrow path to the left of a house to reach its driveway. Go left along the drive until it finally ends at a road. *(1 mile)*

⑤ Cross the road and continue on a path opposite and soon cross a drive. Press on ahead along the waymarked path and fork left on a narrow path 90 yards after rounding a left bend. At a drive, turn right for 12 yards before going left and continuing on the narrow path. In 80 yards turn right and follow the well-signed path as it passes the old house of **Henley Park**, in trees to your right. Maintain direction and after passing through two kissing gates, cross a stile on your left. Now turn right along a field edge and fork left on a downhill cart track that soon brings you to a crossing track. Go over the crossing track to reach a large field, which you cross. At the far side turn left along its edge and ignore a stile on your right. Continue along the field edge and cross a stile in its bottom

corner. Press on along the edge of a meadow and cross a bridge over a stream to soon meet the A323 where the way is left alongside the road to reach the **Duke of Normandy** public house. *(2 miles)*

⑥ Having been refreshed, continue alongside the road and when opposite **Chapel Farm** go left over a stile and continue on a wide cart track through a field. Enter a meadow at the far side and continue ahead on a narrow path where you cross a stile by woodland. Press on ahead and cross an unusual brick footbridge over a brook. Keep ahead and cross another stile and continue up a short rise to meet our earlier path. Turn left through the kissing gate and then go right immediately after passing through the second gate. Press on now to meet the A324. *(1 mile)*

⑦ Turn right along the road and when opposite the main works entrance to **Henley Park** go left on a woodland path. In 10 yards turn right and in a further 10 yards fork left. Now continue ahead along a wide path where you soon ignore a right fork and later tracks to left and right. Some 25 yards before a wire gate bars the way, fork right on a narrower path to meet the bank of **Henleypark Lake**. Continue between rhododendron bushes at the water's edge and cross a concrete bridge to reach a barrier and soon fork right over a wooden bridge to meet a vehicle barrier. (³/₄ mile)

⑧ Press on ahead along the track opposite and pass through a kissing gate. Now remain on this pleasant path as it leads you through woodland and between fields. Finally cross a stile and re-enter woodland to meet a wide crossing track in 10 yards. Turn right along this track until 50 yards after passing **Duchies Cottage** it meets a junction of tracks. Ignore a footpath ahead of you and turn left along the wide track to reach another junction of tracks by the gates of **Pirbright Lodge**. (1 mile)

⑨ Turn right along the lane now and, after passing the gates to **The Manor House**, fork left on a signed path. Follow the path and cross the right-hand side of two small fields to reach a road. Turn right along the road and pass by **St Michael's**

**church**. As you near the end of the graveyard, you will see a large granite stone that marks Sir Henry Morton Stanley's grave.

*This is the Stanley that uttered those immortal words, 'Dr Livingstone, I presume.' After he found Dr Livingstone in the African jungle 1871, they went on to discover Lake Tanganyika together. Stanley Falls, Stanley Pool and Stanleyville (all now renamed) in Zaire were named in his honour. The inscription 'Bula Matari' is the name given to him by his African porters. He spent his last years living quietly in Pirbright with his wife. His wish was to be buried next to Livingstone in Westminster Abbey but this was refused.*

Press on along the lane to reach the village green at **Pirbright** and the end of this terrific walk. (1 mile)

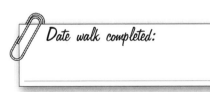
Date walk completed:

# WOOD STREET VILLAGE, WANBOROUGH AND PUTTENHAM

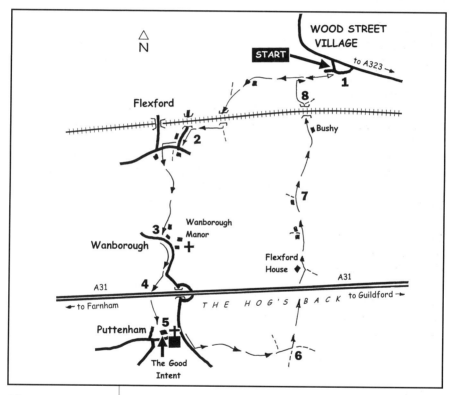

**Distance:**
7¼ miles

**Starting point:**
Wood Street Village green. GR: 954510

Map: OS Landranger 186 Aldershot & Guildford, Camberley & Haslemere

**How to get there:** *Follow the A323 west for ½ mile from the A3 at Guildford and then turn left at a roundabout onto a minor road signposted to the village. The green will be found on your left at the western end of the village.*

ST BARTHOLOMEW'S AT WANBOROUGH IS ONE OF THE OLDEST AND SMALLEST CHURCHES IN SURREY

*T*his enjoyable circuit begins at the pristine green at Wood Street Village where well-kept paths across Backside Common are followed. The way skirts Flexford and joins a field path with extensive views, leading you to the pretty hamlet of Wanborough where a lovely grouping of manor house, church and tithe barn is discovered. Leaving this charming setting, the route begins the easy climb to the top of the Hog's Back where the panoramic views are stunning. Soon the walk descends the ridge's southern slopes to meet the ancient village of Puttenham, the Good Intent pub and the halfway point of the route.

From Puttenham the way follows a short section of the North Downs Way before turning north and re-crossing the Hog's Back. Now with fantastic views ahead, the circuit follows a glorious track that offers easy walking and brings you back to Wood Street Village.

Puttenham is tucked under the southern slopes of the Hog's Back and until recently was known as a hop growing area. In the main street, near the church, is the 16th century pub called the **Good Intent** – a rather promising name don't you think? This is a popular spot with walkers as the North Downs Way passes the door. The interior is welcoming and made cosy in the colder winter months by a large inglenook fireplace while during the summer you may choose to sit in the small garden. There is a good selection of food and if you happen to call by on a Wednesday evening you will find fish and chips being served in paper to either eat in or take away. The landlord is obviously enthusiastic about malt whiskies, as there are around 50 to choose from, so if you share the same passion you will be in heaven. Beers on offer include Courage Best, Young's Bitter, Theakston's Old Peculier, Greene King Abbot Ale and Adnam's Broadside.

**Opening times** *are from 11 am to 2.30 pm and 6 pm to 11 pm Monday to Friday, 11 am to 11 pm on Saturday and 12 noon to 10.30 pm on Sunday. Cooked food is served each lunchtime and during the evenings from Tuesday to Saturday. Booking is required if you are in a party of over six people. Telephone: 01483 810387.*

## The Walk

① From the western end of the village green, walk along **White Hart Lane** where you soon pass the **White Hart** pub. Take time to look at the low wall surmounted by a magnificent metalwork frieze made by a skilled local blacksmith. When the lane ends, press on along an all weather horse ride across **Backside Common**. Pass a cricket pitch and ignore side turnings. When you reach farm buildings to your left, continue ahead to go over the farm drive where the path passes through very pleasant woodland and is soon joined by another from the right. Press on along the path as it goes under a railway bridge. Now ignore a footpath in front of you and continue rightwards along the bridleway that remains parallel to the railway to soon meet a drive. *(1½ miles)*

② Go ahead along the driveway to soon meet a T-junction. Here turn right along the road and 100 yards before meeting a road junction turn left over a stile beside a field gate. Cross a second and a third stile to meet a field edge. The way is diagonally left across the centre of this field to meet a directional post at the far side. Now continue alongside a hedgerow on the left side of the field to meet a stile. Cross the stile and skirt the left side of the field, passing a fine barn conversion before meeting a road by cottages. (1 mile)

③ Go left along the road and soon, at a small road junction, you may wish to take a small diversion leftwards to see **Wanborough's** tithe barn, church and manor house.

*St Bartholomew's church is one of the smallest and oldest churches in Surrey. Originally built around*

*1060, it was restored during the 13th century but fell into disuse after the Civil War and stood neglected before becoming a stable and later a carpenter's workshop. Restored again in 1861, it has remained as it was first intended. Almost out of sight behind it is 17th century Wanborough Manor, once owned by Sir Algernon West, private secretary to Prime Minister Gladstone, who held occasional cabinet meetings here. During the Second World War the house became the secret training ground*

THE GOOD INTENT IS IN PUTTENHAM'S MAIN STREET

*for SOE operatives. The large tithe barn in this group is 15th century.*

The way continues alongside the road towards the ridge of the **Hog's Back**. At a sharp bend in the road, go right over a stile and press on diagonally half right through a large field to meet a stile in the top edge. (¹/₂ mile)

④ Go over the stile and cross the busy A31 dual carriageway with caution and meet the entrance to a nursing home. Go right along the carriageway for 25 yards before turning left on a signposted bridleway. Maintain direction ahead to meet a stony farm track and later a lane where you pass a school to join **Puttenham's** main street. Turn left here and in yards you meet the **Good Intent**. (¹/₂ mile)

⑤ The route continues along the main street where you pass the **church of St John the Baptist** to reach a T-junction. Here turn right and, when opposite the **Jolly Farmer**, a Harvester inn, turn left and continue along a broad track signposted as the **North Downs Way**. Pass a couple of cottages and the rear of **Puttenham Golf Club** clubhouse. After passing a large barn and a small cottage, keep left on the main track and at a second fork by **Greyfriars Farm** keep ahead on the main track. Beyond a group of cottages by

**Monks Grove Farm**, ignore a footpath on your left, but soon, at a large junction of bridleways, leave the **North Downs Way** by turning left along a bridleway. *(1¹/₄ miles)*

⑥ The bridleway rises and takes you to the top of the **Hog's Back** where, again with caution, you should cross diagonally left over the first carriageway to the central reservation before going ahead over the second carriageway to meet a stile beside a bus stop.

*The busy A31 dual carriageway follows the course of the Neolithic Old Hoar Way that ran along the ridge of the Hog's Back, while below the southern slopes was the Old Road – later called the Pilgrims' Way and more recently adopted as the North Downs Way.*

Go over this stile and two more ahead of you to reach a ribbon of trees. Pass through these and cross a private drive to meet a farm drive. Turn left and keep to this very pleasant drive, admiring the superb rural views, until it turns to the left by **Flexford Farm**. *(1¹/₄ miles)*

⑦ Maintain direction ahead here along a track beside a large field to eventually meet the ornate gates of a newly built house named **Bushy**. Don't be intimidated by the CCTV etc., but pass through a wrought

**THE VIEW OVER WANBOROUGH FROM THE HOG'S BACK**

iron pedestrian gate and continue along the drive to reach and pass through a kissing gate. Press on through woodland to soon meet a junction of tracks where you should go ahead and pass under a railway bridge to meet a T-junction. (¹/₂ mile)

⑧ Turn left here along an all weather horse ride that passes through the pleasant woodland of **Backside Common** and alongside a cricket pitch. At a broad crossing track turn right, and at a second crossing track behind the cricket pavilion turn right again. Now follow this path as you retrace your steps to pass the **White Hart** pub and reach the green at **Wood Street Village** and the end of this great walk. (³/₄ mile)

*Date walk completed:*

# CHOBHAM, SOW MOOR AND BURROWHILL

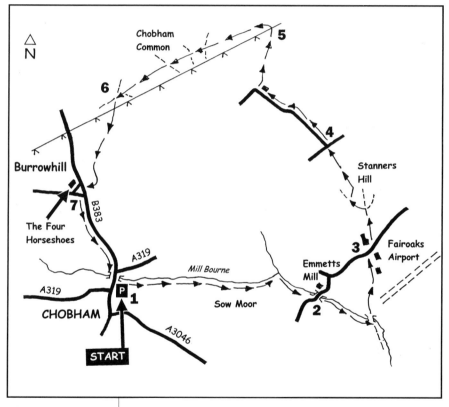

**Distance:**
7 miles

**Starting point:**
The free car park at the north end of Chobham High Street. GR: 974618

Map: OS Landranger 186 Aldershot & Guildford, Camberley & Haslemere

**How to get there:** Chobham is 5 miles south-west of junction 11 of the M25.

THE ROUTE FOLLOWS THIS LOVELY SANDY TRACK ACROSS THE EXPANSE OF CHOBHAM COMMON

*S*tarting from Chobham High Street, this splendid walk winds its way through the wildflower meadows of Sow Moor as it follows the little Mill Bourne stream to Emmetts Mill. During late summer the air is filled with the scent of Himalayan balsam that lines the water's edge as the circuit makes its way to Fairoaks Airport where the path goes surprisingly close to the end of the runway. Heading north now, the way passes through the oak and birch woodland of Stanners Hill as it makes its way to Chobham Common.

As the route reaches the common it follows a lovely sandy track across this Site of Special Scientific Interest, where there are far-reaching views. The Four Horseshoes by Burrowhill's village green, although situated towards the end of the walk, makes a great place to stop and take on refreshment. A short walk alongside a pleasant road brings you back to Chobham and the end of this varied ramble.

On the edge of the vast heathland of Chobham Common lies Burrowhill, a hamlet to the north of Chobham. Although almost a suburb of its larger neighbour, it manages to retain its own identity, helped in no small part by the triangular village green fronted by a blacksmith's forge and the **Four Horseshoes**. This picture-book pub is a gem and deserves a visit. Part of the building is grade II listed while another part was at one time a mortuary; I'll leave you to guess which part is which. The food is good and delivered in generous proportions while the beers, which include Brakspear's Best, Ansells Bitter and John Smith's Smooth, are well kept. The pumps also deliver Guinness, Foster's and Kronenbourg 1664 lagers plus Strongbow and Aldermaster cider.

*Opening times are from 11 am to 11 pm on Monday to Saturday and 12 noon to 10.30 pm on Sunday. Cooked food is available from 12 noon to 3 pm and 7 pm to 9 pm (Sunday 12 noon to 4 pm only). Telephone: 01276 857581.*

# The Walk

① Go to the car park entrance and take the path signposted to **Emmetts Mill**. After passing the side of the car park the path bears left over a grassy area to reach the bank of the **Mill Bourne**. Now continue rightwards through a series of wildflower meadows on a path that remains parallel to the bank of the stream. Finally cross a stile and go ahead under power cables and soon go over a second stile and farm track and continue through a field gate on the path signposted to **Emmetts Mill**. Later cross a stile and when the path bears right, ignore a wooden bridge to your left and remain on the path. Cross another stile and press on ahead along a narrower path where you cross two wooden bridges to reach a lane. *(1¹/₂ miles)*

② Turn left along the lane and just as you reach a humpback bridge with **Emmetts Mill** beyond, turn right on a path signed as footpath 113. At a T-junction, turn left and soon pass the end of the runway of **Fairoaks Airfield**. Continue past airport buildings and along a drive to meet a road. *(1 mile)*

*A watermill has stood on this site for over 500 years. Emmetts Mill is named after Richard Emmett who built his mill here in the late 16th century. The present mill building was erected in 1701 and is now a private residence of some proportion although it can't quite hide its industrial past.*

③ Turn right alongside the road and in 80 yards turn left on a bridleway signposted along a private road. The first house you pass contains an interesting faced stone, purportedly coming from the old Waterloo Bridge. Keep left at a fork in the road and, after passing a couple of houses, fork right on a bridleway that goes uphill through pleasant woodland. At the crest of the rise fork left and continue on the bridleway to reach the rear of a couple of houses. Bear right here and remain on the bridleway as it leads you through more peaceful woodland to reach a road. *(1 mile)*

④ Now go ahead along **Gracious Pond Road** opposite and, when finally by a house named **The White Cottage** on a tight left bend, turn right on a track. Pass by a vehicle barrier and go ahead on a wide track through trees. Continue over a crossing track in 30 yards and 60 yards later bear left at a fork. Keep to this path as it leads you through fine stands of pine until you reach the top of an incline by a marker post. Here turn left on a wide sandy crossing track and pass under power cables. *(1 mile)*

*Chobham Common, an SSSI and a National Nature Reserve, is one of*

THE FOUR HORSESHOES OCCUPIES A PLEASANT SPOT BESIDE THE VILLAGE GREEN

the finest heathland areas in Britain. *The heath, which has around 300 species of flowers, is the best place in Britain to view the wide variety of bees, wasps, ladybirds, 29 species of butterflies and 22 species of dragonflies that live here. On top of all of this are the 100 species of birds and 21 species of animals that have been recorded. It sounds as if you can't put your foot down without treading on them, but I have to say that the inhabitants here are very clever in evading human incursions.*

⑤ Remain ahead when a track comes in from your left and in 25 yards bear left by a marker post. Keep to this fine track now as it remains parallel to a line of power cables. Later, at the crest of a hill by a wide crossing track, keep ahead. In 100 yards another path joins the track from the right and our track goes downhill between trees to meet a bridleway on your left. *(1 mile)*

⑥ Go left here along the bridleway and as the path narrows it soon passes under the power cables. Keep ahead and in 80 yards a field will be seen through the trees on your right. Go over a crossing track to finally meet a large junction of tracks by an electricity sub-station. Go ahead along the bridleway that passes close to the sub-station and soon meet a tarmac drive. Remain on this drive now as it soon bends right and brings you to the B383 with **Burrowhill's** village green and the **Four Horseshoes** pub beyond. *(³/₄ mile)*

⑦ After refreshing yourself, the way continues across the green with the pub at your back. Cross **Windlesham Road** and continue along the right-hand pavement beside the B383. After passing the junction with the A319 the path crosses the **Mill Bourne**. At the end of railings go left across the road to **Cannon Corner** and turn left again to reach the car park entrance and the end of the walk. *(³/₄ mile)*

There are plenty of refreshment places here, including the popular **Sun Inn** in **Chobham High Street**.

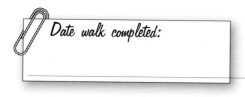

*Date walk completed:*

# SIDNEY WOOD, THE SUSSEX BORDER PATH AND ALFOLD BARS

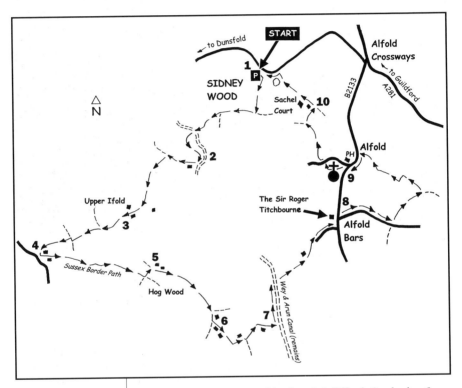

**Distance:** 9¹/₄ miles

**Starting point:** Car park in Sidney Wood. GR: 026351

**Map:** OS Landranger 186 Aldershot & Guildford, Camberley & Haslemere

**How to get there:** Sidney Wood car park is 1 mile west of the A281 on a lane that links Alfold Crossways to Dunsfold.

THE PRETTY APPROACH TO ST NICHOLAS'S CHURCH AT ALFORD PASSES BETWEEN THE VILLAGE STOCKS
AND CENTURIES OLD COTTAGES

*T*his glorious walk starts in Sidney Wood, a remnant of the ancient
forest that once covered this area. The route soon discovers the
remains of the Wey and Arun Canal and the indistinct site of an
ancient glassworks in the forest. After passing the small community of
Upper Ifold on a quiet track, the way turns east by Dungate Farm and
from here it continues amid majestic woodland that is carpeted by
springtime wildflowers and cut through by small streams.

The circuit enters Sussex for a short while and continues along the
towpath of the defunct canal before turning into Alfold Bars to meet
the Sir Roger Tichbourne pub. From here the trail leaves the village on
a quiet lane, then turns onto a wonderful cart track through elevated
fields that offer panoramic views over the countryside. Soon it reaches
Alfold, where it passes ancient St Nicholas's church before crossing
more scenic fields and rejoining Sidney Wood.

The **Sir Roger Tichbourne** sits on the Surrey/Sussex border in Alfold Bars. Although much older, the pub is named after a gentleman who went missing, presumed drowned, after a shipwreck in 1854, only to later reappear. It was soon discovered that this was in fact an impostor and he was brought to trial in 1865 in what became the longest court case of its time. This lovely country pub offers simple no frills food that ranges from the 'Sir Roger' mixed grill, fish and chips, jacket potatoes, ploughman's, baguettes and sandwiches, all of which are served in ample quantities. The pumps deliver a good selection of beers that include Sussex Best and Badger Best as well as Guinness, cider and lagers. There is plenty of room in the sprawling garden for eating outside on fine days, while for those wishing to extend their stay the pub also has a caravan and camping site attached.

*Opening times are from 12 noon to 3 pm and 6 pm to 11 pm on Monday to Saturday and from 12 noon to 2 pm and 7 pm to 10.30 pm on Sunday. Cooked food is available from 12 noon to 2 pm and 7 pm to 9 pm each day. Booking is not necessary. Telephone: 01403 752377.*

## The Walk

*Sidney Wood lies in the fold country and contains evidence of medieval glassmaking for which the area is famed. It is thought that the French glassmaker Jean Carré worked here in these woods where many pieces of old glass have been found. He was responsible for introducing glassmaking from Lorraine into this country. He died in 1572 towards the end of the area's glassmaking heyday and is buried by St Nicholas's church in Alfold.*

① From the car park, continue along the wide track that led you to the parking area. Keep to the track as it bends sharply right and soon pass the paddocks of an isolated house. When the track bends left, you should keep ahead on a path that leads you through trees. After zigzagging between trees you will cross the defunct **Wey and Arun Canal**. Keep ahead along the path as it narrows and passes through a dell and follow it when it turns left to meet the old towpath of the canal. Here are the indistinct remains of the ancient glassworks. (*1 mile*)

② Turn right along the towpath to soon meet a driveway by a house named **Sidney Court**. Turn right here along a drive and when this goes into a dip our way is left along a drive that leads to **Upper Ifold**

**Farm**. After passing the farm and a couple of houses that form **Upper Ifold**, ignore a path to your right and keep ahead on the drive. At a fork by **The Barn House**, keep ahead on a bridleway along a farm track and soon, as it bends right, ignore a path on your right and keep ahead along the bridleway. *(1 mile)*

③ Now remain on the bridleway as it leads you through fine woodland to meet a forest track. Turn right here for 10 yards before turning left and continuing on the bridleway to

finally meet the buildings of **Dungate Farm**. *(³/₄ mile)*

④ Now turn left and pass the old farmhouse and continue between a large barn and **The Old Milking Parlour**, which has been transformed into a cottage. Here our way joins the **Sussex Border Path**, which we now follow for nearly 2 miles. The route continues ahead through a field gate and along the left side of a field. Cross a stile at the far end of the field and enter glorious woodland where you ignore a path on your immediate right. Maintain

THE SIR ROGER TICHBOURNE IS A TYPICAL OLD VILLAGE PUB WITH LOW BEAMS

direction ahead and in 150 yards turn left by a **Sussex Border Path** sign and right in a further 30 yards. Ignore side paths now as our way follows the line of an ancient low bank and ditch through the woodland.

*Most of these banks and ditches date back to Anglo-Saxon times and were boundary markers.*

The path passes through a pretty valley and crosses a woodland stream. Still following the bank and ditch, our way continues through another small valley cut through by a stream. Remain on the **Sussex Border Path** and at a wide grassy crossing track, turn left and in 90 yards meet another wide crossing track. Continue over this track on the signed path to meet a T-junction with a field ahead. *(1 mile)*

⑤ Turn right here to soon meet a driveway, which you now follow. Ignore a **Sussex Border Path** sign on your left when by a bungalow named **Forest View**, but in 200 yards, after passing over a low causeway, leave this track by bearing left on a bridleway that brings you to another driveway. *(1 mile)*

⑥ Press on along this second driveway and keep to it at a sharp left bend. When alongside the entrance to **Lakeside Farm**, go right and then left along a rough track

named **Ifold Bridge Lane**. Before long it crosses a river where you go over a stile and continue until 10 yards after passing a house named **Southland** you will rejoin the towpath of the **Wey and Arun Canal**. *(³/₄ mile)*

⑦ Turn left along the towpath until at a crossing track you rejoin the **Sussex Border Path**. Turn right here and continue on a tree-lined path. When a gate bars the way at a crossing path, continue ahead through the gate to meet the buildings of **Oakhurst Farm**. Keep ahead here along the farm drive and ignore a left fork. The drive leads you to a residential road where you press on to meet a T-junction. Turn left along the road and within yards you will reach the **Sir Roger Tichbourne** and welcome refreshment. *(1 mile)*

⑧ After suitable refreshment, cross the road and continue along **Pig Bush Lane** opposite. At the top of a rise by the gateway to **Songhurst Place**, we finally leave the **Sussex Border Path** by turning left through a field gate. The route is now along a wonderful cart track through fields with panoramic views. At the crest of a rise by a large water tank and a marker post, you should turn left on a path that skirts a field. Soon, go right over a stile and continue along the right-hand side of another field and as this ends press on ahead along the left side of the next field to reach a drive. Turn right along the drive and soon fork left on a signposted footpath between paddocks. Press on through woodland to join a gravel path that brings you to a road by **Alford chapel**. Turn left here and soon bear right by the **Crown** pub to reach the approach to **St Nicholas's church**. *(1¹/₄ miles)*

*St Nicholas's church is Norman and retains many ancient features including a Norman font, 16th century beams, an Elizabethan pulpit and some fragments of 17th century Flemish glass in the east window. Jean Carré, the famous glassmaker, is buried close to the war memorial where a plaque marks the spot.*

⑨ Pass the village stocks and enter the churchyard. The circuit continues to the right of the church on a path that curves right to meet a lane. Turn left along the lane and ignore a path on your right. At a left bend in the lane by the gateway to a house named **Bucklands**, turn right on a fenced path. Cross a stile and continue along the left side of a field to go over a stile in the far corner. Continue ahead over the next field where you cross stiles and a farm track and enter a third field. Here aim for a stile between oak trees but do not cross it. Bear right now and go over a stile in the field edge 80 yards to the right of a house. *(³/₄ mile)*

⑩ Turn left along a drive and when it meets a T-junction with another turn right and pass between a pond and the houses of the **Springbok Estate** – a peaceful place for retired merchant seamen. At the end of this housing, ignore a bridleway to your left and continue rightwards along the drive to meet a road. Turn left here to return to the entrance to **Sidney Wood** car park. *(³/₄ mile)*

Date walk completed:

# SHAMLEY GREEN, THE GREENSAND WAY AND HASCOMBE

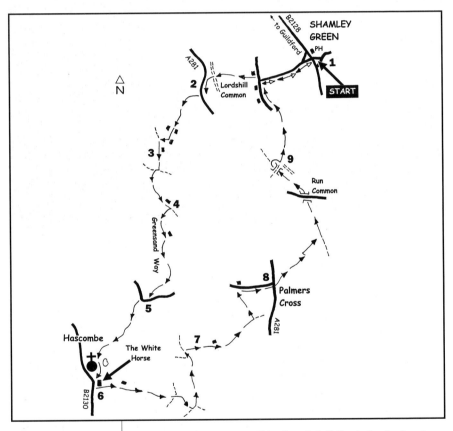

**Distance:**
10 miles

**Starting point:**
Shamley Green
village pond.
GR: 033437

**Map: OS Landranger 186 Aldershot & Guildford, Camberley & Haslemere**

**How to get there:** Shamley Green is 4 miles south of Guildford on the B2128. Park at the roadside near the pond, which is close to the Red Lion pub.

A PASTORAL SCENE FROM THE GREENSAND WAY, ALONG THE SLOPES OF HASCOMBE HILL

Starting off by Shamley Green's pretty duck pond and passing the lovely cricket pitch, this wonderful circuit soon crosses the former Wey and Arun Canal to bring you to the superb scenery below the wooded slopes of Thorncombe Park. The route follows a section of the Greensand Way that leads you over beautiful rolling countryside and through the majestic trees that cover Hascombe Hill before descending to Hascombe where you pass another appealing pond to reach the turning point by the White Horse pub.

Leaving Hascombe behind, the walk continues along easily followed paths and tracks with panoramic views. After crossing pleasant fields, the route meets up with the bed of an old railway that is a haven for wildlife and forms a part of the Downs Link path. The way follows this path for a while before continuing along a quiet lane as it heads back to Shamley Green.

The oldest part of the strung-out village of Hascombe is clustered around St Peter's church and comprises a picturesque grouping of rose adorned cottages, the pretty village pond and the **White Horse**. The 16th century pub once stood at the junction of two old roads and has a long tradition of providing sustenance for travellers. The Greensand Way long distance path now passes its door and walkers on the route find it makes a superb place to stop for refreshment. The food is served in generous helpings and ranges from sandwiches, ploughman's and homemade burgers to a more exotic roast half guinea fowl dish from the à la carte menu in the restaurant. The pumps deliver Harvey's Sussex, Adnam's Best and Courage Director's as well as stout and the usual lagers. There is space for all during the summer months in the lovely garden.

**Opening times** *are from 11 am to 3 pm and 5.30 pm to 11 pm during the week, 11 am to 11 pm on Saturday and 12 noon to 10.30 pm on Sunday. Cooked food is available from 12 noon to 2.20 pm and 7 pm to 10 pm (Sunday 9.30 pm). Booking for an à la carte meal is essential. Telephone: 01483 208258.*

# The Walk

① From the village pond, cross the B2128 and, with the **Red Lion** pub behind you, pass to the left of the village cricket pitch. Continue ahead along **Hullbrook Lane** and at a T-junction turn right and in 25 yards go left on a footpath alongside a house. The path passes between fields and brings you to the **River Wey South Branch**. Cross the river and pass by the indistinct remains of the **Wey and Arun Canal** and continue ahead under a bridge to soon meet a road. *(1 mile)*

*Along the route are a couple of*

*sections of the defunct Wey and Arun Canal, dubbed 'London's lost route to the sea'. Built in 1816 towards the end of the canal building boom, it was thought that a direct route from London to the south coast would avoid the need for shipping to circumnavigate Kent at the risk of being sunk by Napoleon's navy. The canal linked the River Wey Navigation to the River Arun and gave London a direct route to the sea while Portsmouth could be reached via the Portsmouth and Arundel Canal that started at Ford. A combination of improved roads and new railways put paid to the canal, which finally closed in 1871.*

② Turn left along the road, pass converted farm buildings and 80 yards later turn right on a tarmac drive signed as a bridleway. Keep to this drive and later ignore a drive on your right. Press on ahead to pass between a stable block and barns. When the drive approaches a couple of farm cottages follow it rightwards and soon meet a T-junction of bridleways. Turn left here and continue along a gravel drive to pass a beautified farm cottage. (1 mile)

③ When the drive ends continue ahead on a bridleway between fields. At a T-junction, turn right and ignore a path on your right in 8 yards. Continue along the bridleway between banks to meet a farm track and press on ahead to pass a house named **Keepers**. In 120 yards, when beside a large barn, turn right along a cart track signposted as the **Greensand Way** long distance path. (¹/₂ mile)

④ Keep to the track as it follows a field edge and brings you to a modern barn. Go ahead here on a concrete drive and in 80 yards look

**THE WHITE HORSE IN HASCOMBE HAS A LOVELY GARDEN WITH RURAL VIEWS**

out for a **GW** sign where you should bear right and pass the rear of a cottage garden. From here maintain direction across a wide grassy area to meet a low **GW** sign by a gravel drive. Go ahead to meet a rising track that brings you to open parkland. Continue ahead along an indistinct track and when this swings to the right, keep ahead on a path through glorious woodland. Later the path narrows and continues alongside a field to reach a lane. *(1 mile)*

⑤ Turn right along the lane and after 30 yards go left on a bridleway. Soon the path divides and you should fork right on an uphill path. At the top of the rise turn left along the **GW** path and at a junction of tracks go right and remain on the **GW** path. Some 25 yards after passing a barn on the crest of the hill you should bear right and continue on a narrow downhill path between banks. Keep ahead at a driveway by a house and ignore a bridleway on your right as you pass through a gateway. Now follow a lane and soon pass the village pond in its idyllic setting. A few yards further brings you to the **White Horse** pub and the halfway point of the circuit. *(1 mile)*

⑥ After taking on refreshment, you should continue on a private drive that runs alongside the pub and beer garden. When the drive develops into a farm track and turns left towards barns, keep ahead on a bridleway that passes to the right of a cottage. As you near the crest of a rise, ignore a path on your right and, a few yards later, go ahead over a crossing track at the crest of the hill. Maintain direction on an eroded downhill path and, at a T-junction by a tennis court, turn left. In 15 yards, by a gate, turn left again and continue along a broad track that passes through woodland before continuing alongside fields with panoramic views. On a downward slope with banks either side, ignore a path on your left, but 120 yards later turn right on a signposted footpath along a field edge. *(1³/₄ miles)*

⑦ Near the end of the field go left on a cart track and in 10 yards turn right and enter a second field. Now continue towards an isolated cottage in the trees ahead of you and, as you near it, bear right on a signed path. Pass the well-preserved cottage and continue along its drive to meet a T-junction. Here turn left along a farm track and after passing between the barns of **Tilsey Farm** keep ahead on a tarmac drive where you pass by a pond. In 30 yards, when confronted by two field gates, go through the left-hand gate and turn left along a field edge. Cross a stile and a wooden bridge at the end of the field and continue along the left side of the next field.

As the field opens out, press on to a stile in the trees ahead of you. Cross the stile and continue through a band of scrub and over an open grassy area to reach a lane by a cottage. The way is now right along the lane to meet the A281. (1¹/₄ miles)

⑧ Cross the main road and continue ahead along the drive to **Whipley Manor**. When the drive swings to the right by a cottage, turn left on a signposted path where in 10 yards you should turn right and continue along a field edge. Cross a stile at the end of the field and continue on a path between trees. Pass through a kissing gate to reach a crossing track. Here, turn left along the straight track that forms a part of the **Downs Link** long distance path and soon pass under a road bridge at **Run Common**. Immediately after going under a second bridge, you should turn right to meet a farm track. (1¹/₄ miles)

*The Downs Link long distance path was created in 1984. Starting at St Martha's Hill, Chilworth, the route links the North Downs Way to the South Downs Way. For most of its length it follows the bed of the railway line that helped put the final nail in the coffin of the Wey and Arun Canal but, just like the canal, it too suffered from underuse and was axed in 1965.*

⑨ Turn left at this track where you will see the depression of the canal bed in the field on your right. In 50 yards bear right along a bridleway that skirts a field and leads to a bridge where you cross a stream. Press on through a coppice to meet a tarmac drive by **Long Common Cottage**. Continue along this pretty drive until after passing **Hullhatch**, an old timber-framed house, you meet a road junction. Turn right here along **Hullbrook Lane** and retrace your steps back to **Shamley Green** and the end of this excellent circuit. (1¹/₄ miles)

*Date walk completed:*

# BLACKHEATH, BROADFORD AND COMPTON

THE MAGNIFICENT WATTS CHAPEL, WITH ITS ART NOUVEAU INTERIOR, IS NOT TO BE MISSED

**Distance:**
13¹/₄ miles

**Starting point:**
The car park near
the Villagers pub at
Blackheath.
GR: 035462

**Map: OS Landranger 186 Aldershot & Guildford, Camberley &**
Haslemere

**How to get there:** Blackheath is 4 miles south-east of
Guildford. Turn off the A248 by Chilworth railway station
and soon turn left at a crossroads. Pass the Villagers pub to
meet a car park at the lane's end.

*A*lthough this varied circuit is the longest in the book, it is one of the easiest to follow. After beginning amongst the tall pines of Blackheath, the route makes its way easily to the Wey & Godalming Navigation at Broadford where it follows the towpath for a while. Soon the route turns west across scenic fields and after passing Loseley Park the old village of Compton and the Harrow Inn are reached.

Leaving Compton behind, the route passes the striking terracotta Watts Chapel and the Watts Gallery, which are both worth a visit. Now following the North Downs Way along tracks with great views, the circuit brings you to the banks of the River Wey just outside Guildford. After crossing the river and passing along a quiet residential road, the route continues through wonderful fields below the Chantries and reaches peaceful woodland concealing the remains of Chilworth's gunpowder mills, from where it is only a short distance back to Blackheath.

 The attractive village of Compton nestles below the southern flank of the Hog's Back and is happily bypassed by the A3 dual carriageway, although the B3000 that forms the main street is busy enough. There is a 900-year-old church and many ancient houses, a couple of which date back almost 500 years. Not quite in that league is the 17th century **Harrow Inn**, a good watering hole that will delight those of you who are food orientated. The wide choice ranges from sandwiches, baguettes, baked potatoes and ploughman's to main courses in the restaurant area that include a dish of natural smoked haddock with cheese sauce on spinach topped with a poached egg – not exactly pub grub. The beers are well kept and include TEA from the local Hog's Back Brewery plus lager and stout. There is seating in the pleasant garden and a patio to the rear.

**Opening times** *are from 11 am to 11 pm on Monday to Saturday and 12 noon to 6 pm on Sunday. Cooked food is available from 12 noon to 3 pm and 6 pm to 10 pm (not Sunday evening).*
*Booking is required if you are in a large group.*
*Telephone: 01483 810379.*

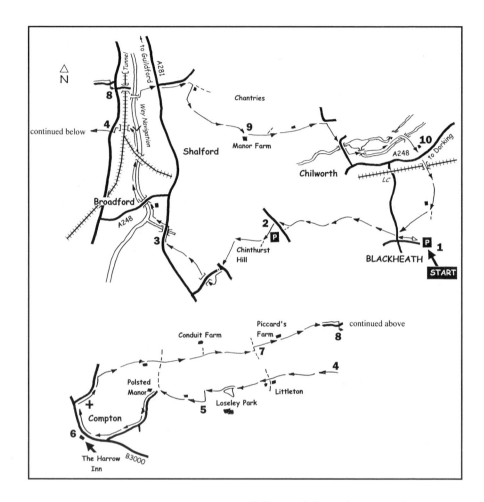

# The Walk

① Walk back along the lane and pass the **Villagers** pub to reach the crossroads. Turn right along the road and 100 yards later go left on a signed bridleway. Go over a crossing track to reach a cart track and follow it leftwards. Pass a house and, when the track ends at a fork, continue on the left fork. When a group of houses are met, press on ahead along the **Downs Link** path. With a road 80 yards ahead of you, bear right on a bridleway to reach the road. *(1¹⁄₄ miles)*

② Cross the road and continue

along the **Downs Link** path. Within yards of passing a car parking area, turn right and remain on the **Downs Link**, later ignoring a stile to your right at a left bend. The path ends at a road junction and you should continue ahead along **Tannery Lane**. A few yards before a road bridge, fork left on the **Downs Link** path. In 20 yards fork right and cross the pedestrian bridge to meet a T-junction. Turn right under the bridge and continue along a straight path to reach a road. (1¼ miles)

③ Go right along the road and turn left on a signed path 80 yards after passing over a canal. Continue on a fenced path to reach a group of cottages where you should keep ahead on a path that goes between modern offices and an old gunpowder store at the canal's edge.

*This canal bank once formed Broadford Wharf and it was from here that gunpowder from the nearby Chilworth mills was loaded onto barges for the journey to London.*

At a road, go left over a bridge and then turn right along the towpath to reach **St Catherine's Lock**. Turn left here along a rough track and pass under a railway bridge to reach a road. (1¼ miles)

④ Turn left along the road and soon go right into a road named **The Ridges**. When this ends, keep ahead on a narrow path. When a drive is met, continue ahead to a road junction by **Pillarbox Cottage**. Press on ahead, cross a stile and maintain direction on a well-defined path through two fields to reach a picturesque lake with thoughtfully placed seats. Keep ahead along a field edge and cross two stiles in quick succession to enter another field. In 50 yards go left with the field edge and continue on a fenced path to meet a rough track. (1¼ miles)

⑤ Go right along the track and when this meets a lane beside a house named **Little Polsted**, continue leftwards along the lane. Later ignore a small road on your left and carry on to reach a large grassy area fronted by houses. Bear right across the grass to reach **Compton's** main street where you continue rightwards to pass the village hall and reach the **Harrow Inn**. (1 mile)

⑥ Leaving the **Harrow Inn** behind, the way continues along the main street before turning right into **Down Lane** where you pass the **Watts Chapel**.

*Compton was the home to George Frederick Watts, a Victorian artist known as 'England's*

*Michelangelo'. He is remembered in the extraordinary chapel designed by his wife and built in 1896 by the villagers. The stunning terracotta building is in the form of a Greek cross and the richly decorated art-nouveau interior is not to be missed. Further along the lane is the Watts Gallery where his work is displayed.*

Press on along the lane and, when beside the **Watts Gallery**, turn right on a sandy track signposted as the **North Downs Way**. This path will now lead you back to the **River**

**Wey** on the outskirts of **Guildford**, with very little need for further instruction other than to remain on the signposted path.
*(2 miles)*

⑦ When the path meets a T-junction with a farm track, turn left and in 80 yards go right along the drive to **Piccard's Farm**. Press on ahead along a cart track after passing farm buildings and in 120 yards keep left at a fork. Finally the path ends at a road where you should continue left to reach a T-junction by the **Olde Ship Inn**.
*(1 mile)*

THE HARROW INN, A VILLAGE PUB WITH A REPUTATION FOR SPLENDID FOOD

⑧ Turn right here and soon turn left into **Ferry Lane**. Pass over a railway bridge and continue downhill to meet the **River Wey**. Go right along its bank and cross a bridge over the river. Soon the path heads away from the water's edge and you should continue over a wide grassy area to reach double gates ahead of you by a road. Press on ahead along a road named **Pilgrims Way**.

*On the left side of this road is a residence named Cyder Cottage. On the line of the old 'Pilgrims' Way', it was originally a pest house (plague hospital) before being converted into cottages. Then called Cyder House Cottages, they remained quite isolated on this once leafy track until the urban sprawl of Guildford caught up with them between the wars and the building became gentrified.*

When the road bends left, fork right along the **North Downs Way** to reach **Chantry Cottage**. Here leave the long distance path by forking right and continuing on an enclosed path to reach another road. Go left along the road and in 40 yards turn left and cross an immense field on a well-trodden path. Maintain direction when a hedgerow is met and continue to a stile near **Manor Farm**. *(1¹/₄ miles)*

⑨ Cross the stile and go left on a well-used path between hedgerows to eventually meet a small lane. Go ahead along the lane for 10 yards before turning right on a fenced path that brings you to the junction of two lanes. Bear right along **Blacksmith Lane** and, after crossing a second bridge, turn left through iron gates beside a small gatehouse.

*This was the entranceway to Chilworth's gunpowder mills that at one time employed 400 people. The granite millstones seen in the woodland were imported from France because of their non-sparking properties. Unlike the stones used for milling corn, these were used vertically as can be seen by their smooth edges.*

Continue along the path and after passing a line of millstones keep left at a fork. At a second fork by a mound of earth, keep right and soon pass the old buildings of the mill to reach a farm lane. Turn right along the lane to meet a road. *(1³/₄ miles)*

*The ruins illustrate how the gunpowder mill was constructed. The missing front walls and roof were made of light materials so that in the event of an explosion, they blew out easily rather than destroy the whole building. Gunpowder production ceased here in 1920.*

ON THE ROUTE

⑩ Cross the road and continue along a lane opposite, signed **Downs Link**. Go ahead on a rising path to the right of white gates to reach a junction of tracks beside **Lingwood House**. Keep on the **Downs Link** path and soon go over a crossing track, staying with the **Downs Link** path as it crosses a second track and passes to the right of a lonely memorial cross commemorating the lives of eight **Blackheath** men who lost their lives in World War I. At a T-junction turn left to soon meet a road and continue left along it to reach a crossroads. Turn left here and retrace your steps past the **Villagers** to the end of this cracking walk. *(1 1/4 miles)*

*Date walk completed:*

# NEWLANDS CORNER, SHERE AND SUTTON ABINGER

THE ROUTE FOLLOWS THE PRETTY TILLING BOURNE INTO THE CENTRE OF SHERE

**Distance:**
12¹/₂ miles

**Starting point:**
The car park at
Newlands Corner.
GR: 044492

Maps: OS Landranger 186 Aldershot & Guildford, Camberley &
Haslemere and 187 Dorking & Reigate, Crawley & Horsham

**How to get there:** The car park is on the A25 south-east
of Guildford.

*T*his invigorating walk starts from the heights of Newlands Corner, one of the county's best-known beauty spots. The circuit begins by descending from the downs to meet the pretty Tilling Bourne, and following its clear waters to Shere to discover one of Surrey's prettiest villages. From here the way is along field paths and passes the outskirts of Gomshall before starting to climb out of the valley. With superb views over the surrounding countryside the route crosses open fields with great views to meet Sutton Abinger.

After welcome refreshment at the Volunteer public house, the walk heads across the Tillingbourne Valley where it passes Paddington Mill and its charming millpond. Now the circuit begins a fairly strenuous climb to reach Hackhurst Downs. Here it follows the North Downs Way long distance path along a level track that will bring you right back to Newlands Corner and the end of this enjoyable excursion in the Surrey Hills.

Nestling in a pretty little valley at Sutton Abinger and well off the beaten track, the **Volunteer** pub requires some seeking out. Starting life as a row of four farm workers' cottages some 300 hundred years ago, it has been skilfully created and the interior retains a traditional country village atmosphere. Its ancestry also explains how the main bar has acquired a double-sided fireplace that gives off a cosy ambience during the colder winter months. The pub enjoys a good reputation for its wide selection of British cheeses and freshly cooked food and majors on speciality fish dishes. The choice of beers includes King and Barnes Sussex Ale, Badger Best, Badger Tanglefoot and a seasonal beer. The peaceful terraced rear garden makes a splendid place in summer to take on fuel before completing the circuit. Booking is only necessary if you wish to dine in the evening.

**Opening times** *are from 11.30 am to 3 pm and 6 pm to 11 pm on Monday to Friday, 11.30 am to 11 pm on Saturday and 12 noon to 10.30 pm on Sunday. Cooked food is available from 12 noon to 2.30 pm and 7 pm to 9.30 pm (Sunday 12 noon to 4 pm only). Telephone: 01306 730798.*

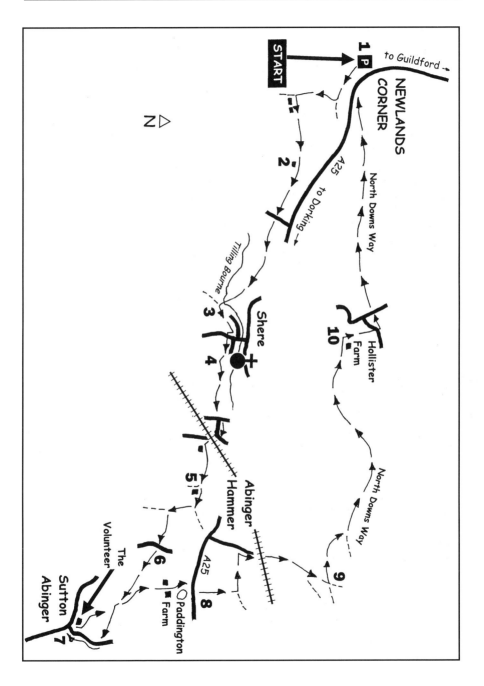

# 🥾 The Walk

① Walk towards the car park entrance to meet a **North Downs Way** directional sign on your right. Ignore the sign and go right here on a downhill stony track. As you enter woodland, ignore a path on your right, but 20 yards later turn right on a track beside a World War II pillbox. Soon meet and follow a farm track that goes between banks. Turn left on a bridleway along another farm track and immediately pass a couple of cottages before continuing between fields. *(1 mile)*

② At an isolated cottage by a directional post, bear right and pass the front of the cottage. Maintain direction along a wide track and in 140 yards fork right along a narrower path where you soon cross a quarry track. Press on here to reach a field and maintain direction ahead to reach a road. Take the farm track opposite and enter another field. Keep ahead, meeting and passing through woodland on a well-trodden path, and at another field maintain direction and continue through woodland to reach a quiet lane. Turn right along the lane and soon cross the **Tilling Bourne** beside a ford. *(1¹/₂ miles)*

③ Pass through a kissing gate on your left and follow a distinct path alongside the stream. At a second gate, keep ahead along a track and pass a second ford. Continue on a tarmac lane beside pretty cottages to reach the centre of **Shere**. Here, if you require refreshment, you will find two pubs to your right and a teashop to your left. At the road junction, cross over and continue through **The Square**, soon passing a war memorial. When alongside the church, the route continues through a gate to the left of a lane named **Church Hill**. *(¹/₂ mile)*

*As you pass St James's church in Shere, give a thought to Christine Carpenter, a local girl who in 1329 wished to prove her obedience to God by becoming an anchoress. This entailed her being walled up in a tiny cell within the north wall of the church. Her only contact with the outside world was via a narrow squint through which food was passed to her, but after three years she pleaded to be let out and the bishop begrudgingly granted her wish. Later she begged to return and it is assumed that she remained there until her death.*

④ The path ends at a large field and you should now turn left along its edge. Keep ahead when it ends and continue on a fenced path that ends at a driveway. Bear left along the drive to meet a road junction. Go ahead here along a road named

High View and then turn right into Tower Hill and pass under a railway bridge. Some 20 yards later, turn left on a bridleway and pass the side of farm buildings and soon to the left of a house. Maintain direction along a well-used path to meet a broad track and continue to the right. *(1 mile)*

⑤ When the track bends sharply right by a house, go left on a narrow signposted bridleway. Turn right when a junction of tracks is met beside the gateway to a house. Continue along a sunken path and

ignore a stile on your right, but 40 yards later go left over a stile and enter a field. Turn right along the field edge and at a marker post in 150 yards turn left directly over the field, passing a line of trees. Cross a stile at the far side and follow a fenced path that skirts a garden and brings you to a lane. *(³/₄ mile)*

⑥ Cross the lane and continue ahead uphill to reach a field and power cables. Keep ahead across the field, following the line of cables. At a second field follow the cables to meet the far side where you should

THE VOLUNTEER NESTLES IN A VALLEY AND HAS A STEEP TERRACED GARDEN

now bear right along the field edge, with a hedgerow to your left. Soon, at the end of the hedgerow and where the field edge bends to the left, go left and continue on a footpath that passes through a hedgerow and crosses diagonally right over another field and towards the buildings of **Raikes Farm**. At the far side meet a lane and turn right along it to reach the **Volunteer** public house. *(1 mile)*

⑦ After visiting the **Volunteer**, go back up the lane and in 50 yards turn left along a track signed as a bridleway. Soon, by gates, bear right on a narrower path to meet a field. Go ahead along the right-hand edge where you meet your earlier path. Go left and in 25 yards turn right on a signposted bridleway. This time ignore the power cables and continue ahead with fabulous views towards the **North Downs**. Now follow the bridleway until you meet the buildings of **Paddington Farm**. Here go left and right between buildings on the farm drive where you soon pass between **Paddington Mill** and its millpond to reach the A25. *(1¼ miles)*

⑧ Cross the A25 to the bridleway opposite and continue between banks to reach a field. Pass through a gate and continue ahead to another at the far side. Go through this and in 50 yards meet a junction of tracks. Turn left here along a broad bridleway and when the track bends sharply right by a gate, continue ahead through the gate. Press on along a field edge to soon meet a lane. Turn right here along the lane and keep left at a fork by cottages where you pass beside farm buildings to reach a railway line. Cross the railway carefully, and continue ahead on a path that takes you to the top of the **North Downs**. Ignore a right forking bridleway as you near the top. *(1½ miles)*

⑨ Near the crest of the hill you will meet kissing gates to left and right on **Blatchford Down**. Go left through the kissing gate and continue along the signed **North Downs Way** long distance path. Now follow the **North Downs Way** signs (some denoted by an acorn sign) until you meet a T-junction by a **Hackhurst Downs** information board. The way continues leftwards, along the long distance path, on a wonderful track that you should remain on until you reach riding stables at **Hollister Farm**. *(2 miles)*

*The North Downs Way long distance path was created in 1978 and is 141 miles long. Starting in Farnham it follows the lower slopes of the Hog's Back before joining the North Downs and continuing along its ridge through Surrey and Kent to meet the coast at Dover.*

THE SUPERB VIEW FROM NEWLANDS CORNER

(10) Follow the track rightwards and at a fork keep ahead. At a second fork continue ahead along the **North Downs Way** to reach a road. Follow the road right for 30 yards before going left on the waymarked path. At a second road, go ahead through a parking area and maintain direction ahead on a broad path. Ignore paths to left and right and keep ahead along the well-trodden long distance path to finally reach the A25. Cross this to meet the car park at **Newlands Corner** and the end of this splendid circuit. (*2 miles*)

The café bar in the car park is open every day during daylight hours, or for the more refined, cream teas are available in the **New Barn Coffee Shop** opposite the car park entrance.

Date walk completed:

# RIPLEY, OLD WOKING AND CARTBRIDGE

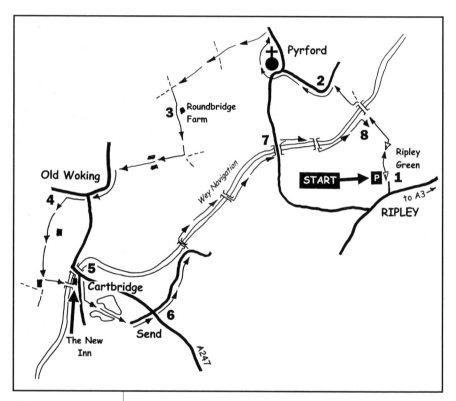

**Distance:**
9³/₄ miles

**Starting point:**
Ripley village green.
GR: 054571

**Maps:** OS Landranger 186 Aldershot & Guildford, Camberley & Haslemere and 187 Dorking & Reigate, Crawley & Horsham

**How to get there:** *Ripley is off the A3 and is 2¹/₂ miles south of junction 10 of the M25. When approaching from the A3, turn right on a narrow lane 80 yards after passing the Half Moon pub and park in the designated area 150 yards ahead.*

THE MOURNFUL REMAINS OF NEWARK PRIORY SEEN ACROSS THE WATER MEADOWS

*T*his interesting walk soon crosses the Wey Navigation at Walsham Gates and heads for Pyrford where it passes the wonderful church of St Nicholas. It's worth a visit just to see the red ochre fresco painted in 1140. The route then heads for Old Woking and continues along its busy little high street before crossing wildlife meadows. The canal is rejoined for a short stretch at Cartbridge and we reach the New Inn, the circuit's halfway point.

The return route continues along pleasant, quiet lanes and footpaths and passes through Send to join the Wey Navigation again. The towpath is now followed for 2 miles through stunning scenery and passes Papercourt and Newark Locks where across the water meadows the stark ruins of Newark Priory will be seen. All too soon Walsham Gates are reached and it is just a short walk back to Ripley village green.

I suspect that most people who drive along the busy A247 on their way to or from Woking miss seeing the picturesque Wey Navigation when they cross it on the newly built bridge at Cartbridge. The **New Inn** is another place easily missed as it is tucked away alongside the bridge and canal. It would be hard to find a more relaxing spot to sit and enjoy a summertime pub lunch than here in the garden that fronts the towpath.

Inside, the comfortable bar areas have beamed ceilings that offer a cosy atmosphere, while from the pumps come Fuller's London Pride, Tetley's, Greene King Abbot Ale and Adnam's. The food is excellent, with starters that include whitebait and a fresh flat mushroom dish, followed by main courses such as chicken and seafood paella, smoked haddock and fresh grilled lemon sole. If your need is for something lighter, then bar snacks are also available.

**Opening times** *are from 11 am to 3 pm and 5 pm to 11 pm on weekdays and all day at weekends. Cooked food is available during each session and, for this, booking is essential during the busy summer months. Telephone: 01483 762736.*

## The Walk

① From the parking area continue along the tarmac lane and follow it leftwards when it bends sharply. After crossing a stream, the lane ends by two houses. Go ahead on a signed footpath between fields to reach **Walsham** weir and gates. Cross the bridge over the rushing waters and follow the path past the lock keeper's house to reach and cross a small bridge on your left. Ignore a signposted footpath ahead of you and bear left to follow a cart track until it reaches a country lane.
*(1 mile)*

*The Wey was not navigable until Sir Richard Weston, the then owner of Sutton Place, built the River Wey Navigation in 1653. The canalised river overcame the fluctuations in water levels and straightened the rather tortuous route the river takes through the fields on its way to Weybridge. The 15-mile-long canal linked Guildford to the Thames and enabled coal to be delivered upstream while farm produce made the return journey. These days, pleasure seekers in colourful narrowboats ply its waters and pass through the twelve locks that are required to overcome the 68-foot rise to Guildford. Sections of the river still meander wildly through the fields.*

② Turn left along the lane and soon after passing **Wheelers Farm** meet a road junction. Turn left along the bending road and at the next bend turn right on a rising footpath through trees to reach the wonderful church at **Pyrford**. Press on to the left of the memorial cross to rejoin the road and continue ahead. Soon after rounding a bend in the road turn left on a bridleway. Go straight over a crossing track and continue with a golf course on either side of the tree-lined path. At a second crossing track, turn left and continue along an avenue of poplar trees to meet the buildings of **Roundbridge Farm**. *(1³/₄ miles)*

③ Pass to the right of the farmhouse and at a small junction of farm tracks go right for 8 yards before bearing left and maintaining your original direction along a tarmac path. After passing the rear of a water treatment works the path meets a junction of tracks. Turn right here and pass a small group of houses before the lane finally ends

THE NEW INN AT CARTBRIDGE OCCUPIES A LOVELY SPOT NEXT TO THE CANAL

at a T-junction. Turn left alongside the road through **Old Woking**. Pass a mini-roundabout and keep ahead until, on your left, you reach the entranceway to a large printing company. *(1¹/₂ miles)*

④ Turn left here over a bridge and in 12 yards fork right over a stile to enter a meadow set aside for wildlife where we leave the hustle and bustle of **Old Woking** behind. Follow the left-hand field edge and ignore a wooden footbridge to your left. Keep ahead by crossing a single plank over a ditch and continue along the left side of the next meadow to reach a football pitch. Maintain direction along the left side to reach a path and pass through woodland. On exiting the woodland, maintain direction ahead through two further meadows to reach the gate of **Fishers Farm**. Ignore a stile ahead of you and turn left along the farm drive. Cross two bridges and at a bend go ahead and cross a footbridge over the **Wey Navigation**. Turn left alongside the canal to reach the A247 road and the front entrance of the **New Inn**. *(1 mile)*

⑤ After suitable refreshment, leave the front door of the pub and with your back to the busy A247 continue along a pleasant residential road. Ignore a footpath signposted to left and right and press on ahead until you meet a driveway opposite

the gates to **Pembroke House**. Go left here and soon continue on a narrow fenced path between two fishing lakes. At the end of the lakes keep ahead to meet a road by the gate of **Hillside Farm**. Turn left along the road to rejoin the A247. *(1 mile)*

⑥ Cross the main road and continue ahead along **Tannery Lane** until you meet up with a line of factories, at the end of which you should turn left and soon cross a footbridge over the canal. Here, quite suddenly, you leave the ugliness of industry and return to the beauties of nature as you turn right alongside the canal. Now follow the towpath to **Papercourt Lock** where you cross a bridge and continue alongside the right bank to finally reach a road. *(1³/₄ miles)*

⑦ Turn left over the road bridge and then immediately right alongside the canal.

*In the fields to your left are the remains of Newark Priory, a 12th century monastery that was abandoned at the Dissolution. On the opposite bank, nearer the road, stood 17th century Newark Mill, a large white weatherboarded building that closed in 1943. After falling into disrepair it was sadly lost to a fire in 1966 and all that remains are the footings and water leat.*

THE LOCK-KEEPER'S HOUSE AT WALSHAM WEIR

*The grouping of brick-built buildings on the site are from the 18th century.*

Cross another bridge at **Newark Lock** and continue along the right bank to finally meet **Walsham gates**. *(1 mile)*

⑧ Turn right beside the weir and retrace your steps along the path between fields to reach a tarmac lane. Now follow the lane until you reach the parking area on **Ripley village green**. *(³/₄ mile)*

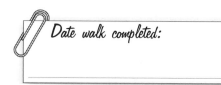

*Date walk completed:*

# FOREST GREEN, OCKLEY AND WALLISWOOOD

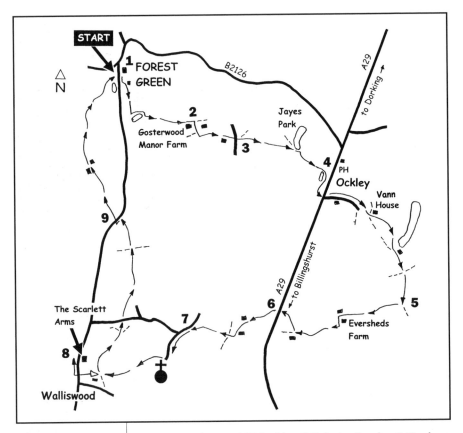

**Distance:**
10¹/₄ mile

**Starting point:**
Forest Green village green.
GR: 124412

**Map:** OS Landranger 187 Dorking & Reigate, Crawley & Horsham

**How to get there:** *Forest Green is 2 miles west of the A29 at Ockley. Park alongside the green near the Parrot pub.*

OCKLEY'S PRETTY VILLAGE POND AND GREEN

*T*his enjoyable circuit starts in the spread-out village of Forest Green and passes ancient farmhouses before crossing the fields of Jayes Park to reach Ockley, with its lovely green lined by topsy-turvy old cottages. Remaining in an eastwardly direction the route goes through the wondrous woodland by Vann Lake and begins to swing south and then west towards Walliswood. The way passes lovely Eversheds Farm before reaching one of Surrey's remotest churches at Okewood. From here the walk continues through peaceful woodland cut through by small rivulets to reach the Scarlett Arms at Walliswood.

After taking on refreshment, we set off northwards, still amidst trees, passing a few houses dotted in tranquil forest clearings. The path continues through a small nature reserve before crossing scenic fields and rejoining the village green at Forest Green.

The small community of Walliswood is fortunately far enough away from the A29 road for it not to be spoilt by modern-day traffic. At the heart of the hamlet is the wonderfully rustic Scarlett Arms pub, a real joy to those who visit. Starting life back in 1620 as farm workers' cottages, the building remained that way for almost 300 years before being converted into a public house, and with inglenook fireplace, stone floors and low beams it just radiates 'olde worlde' charm. From behind the bar come King & Barnes Sussex and Badger Tanglefoot bitters, plus cider, lagers and Guinness. The kitchen provides homemade food in good proportions, ranging from simple snacks to dishes from the more adventurous à la carte menu.

**Opening times** *are from 11 am to 2.30 pm and 5.30 pm to 11 pm on weekdays and Saturdays. Sunday opening is from 12 noon to 3 pm and 7 pm to 10.30 pm. Booking is advisable if you wish to order a cooked meal. Telephone: 01306 627243.*

---

**Note:** The route is through a part of the Weald where the clay soils will become rather sticky during wet winters.

① From the **Parrot** pub walk south along the road and 25 yards after passing the village hall turn left on a signed path along a short tarmac drive. Within yards bear right across the front of a group of houses and continue alongside the garden of a white cottage to cross a stile. Now go right along the right side of a field to meet its corner. Here continue left along the field edge and at the end of a pond turn right to reach a drive. Turn left along the drive and pass the farmhouse of **Gosterwood Manor Farm** to reach

a very large barn on your left. *(1 mile)*

② Soon after passing the barn turn right on a signposted path beside a house and cross a stile. Ignore a path on your right and go ahead along the right-hand field edge to the corner. Now turn left along its edge to meet and cross a stile on your right. Go left now along a broad path, cross a drive and continue ahead on a narrower path. Cross a stile and bear left along a second drive where you pass the rustic buildings of **Volvens Farm** to reach a lane. *($^1/_2$ mile)*

③ Cross the lane and continue, ignoring a left fork when opposite a field gate. Keep ahead, reaching and crossing a stile. Now fork left over a small wooden bridge and in

12 yards cross a stile on your right. Go over a large field, making for a stile just to the left of a group of trees in the corner. Cross the stile and a bridge at the end of a scenic lake to reach a field. Turn right along the field edge and at a protruding section fork left across the open field, aiming just to the right of a house with a low roof, to meet the long village green at **Ockley**. *(1 mile)*

*The name Ockley is derived from the Saxon 'Occa's Lea', meaning Occa's clearing in the wood.*

*During Saxon times this whole area was heavily forested, as the nearby hamlet names of Walliswood and Okewood testify.*

④ If you are in need of refreshment at this stage of the walk, ahead and left is a fine old pub. The way now continues rightwards alongside the pond where we join a rough track. After passing the football and cricket pitches the track swings left to pass the pavilion and brings you to the A29.

*Look at the A29 here in Ockley,*

THE SCARLETT ARMS IN WALLISWOOD MAKES THE PERFECT SPOT FOR REFRESHMENT

*for its straightness gives the clue to its origins. Underneath lies Stane Street, the Roman road that linked Chichester to London.*

Go ahead along **Friday Street** and continue through a gateway by **Vann Cottage**. Stay on the drive until you reach the ornate gates of **Vann House**. Here follow a fenced bridleway to the right of these gates and soon enter **Vann Lake Nature Reserve**. Go ahead here to reach a fork where you should bear left and follow the blue arrowed bridleway. Cross a wooden bridge and fork right uphill. Ignore a crossing track at the top of the rise and continue ahead until you meet a distinct bridleway, signed with a blue arrow, on your right. *(1¹/₂ miles)*

⑤ Turn right along this bridleway to soon reach the edge of the woodland and a T-junction. Turn right along the bridleway as it remains close to a field on your right. On leaving the woodland, press on ahead to meet the buildings of **Eversheds Farm**. Continue along the farm drive and pass the magnificent Georgian farmhouse. As you pass the rear of the building, you will notice that it actually started life during Tudor times. Keep to the drive and, after passing through a shallow depression, ignore a left fork. As you approach farm buildings to your left, bear right at a fork and

continue along a wide track to soon reach the A29 main road. *(1¹/₄ miles)*

⑥ Cross the main road, pass through a gateway and continue along a shingle drive until it ends at a house. Bear left here and follow a fenced bridleway, at the end of which go through a gate to meet a farm track by buildings. Turn right here and pass through a second gate. In 12 yards fork right to meet a stile beside a field gate. Ignore a gated bridleway on your right and a footpath forking to your left. Cross the stile and press on ahead over the centre of the field and, when near the other side, bear slightly left along a line of oak trees to reach a lane. *(1 mile)*

⑦ Turn left along the lane and left again into a charming cul-de-sac that ends in a dell by the **church of St John the Baptist**, surely the remotest in the county. Enter the churchyard and immediately turn right on a path beside a brook. Soon cross two small wooden bridges and continue ahead to a third, ignoring one to your right. Press on ahead uphill, with a deep gully to your left. As the edge of the woodland is reached, a path joins us from the right and within yards we meet a field gate. Follow the path rightwards here and soon pass the rear of houses. Keep ahead at two small crossing paths and continue on a fenced path to reach a road where you will discover the **Scarlett Arms** a few yards to your right. *(1 mile)*

⑧ After refreshment, return to the kissing gate and head back along the fenced path. Some 25 yards after the end of the fencing, turn left on a signed crossing path. Maintain direction on this lovely path, passing several lonely houses in the forest. Finally, at a large junction of tracks, maintain direction ahead on a signed footpath to soon meet a road. Cross the road, pass through a gate and continue along the right side of a field that forms a part of **Wallis Wood Nature Reserve**. Press on along the side of a second field and exit via a kissing gate to meet a T-junction. Now turn left along a wide path with fields on either side. When this finally ends at a T-junction, go ahead through a narrow gate and cross a field to a stile opposite. Pass along the left side of a second field to reach a road. *(1½ miles)*

⑨ Turn left along the road for 25 yards before turning right over a stile. Now follow the yellow arrows as they direct you through the fields ahead. Cross the centre of the field to a stile and pass through a strip of woodland and over a wooden bridge. Keep ahead along the left side of the next field and cross two stiles in quick succession. Press on across this and another field in the direction of stabling. Pass close to the right-hand side of the stables to reach a small black barn. The path continues along its left side where you pass through a couple of paddocks. Still following the yellow arrows, finally cross a stile under a large spreading oak tree to meet a concrete farm drive. Turn right along the drive and before long you will find yourself back at **Forest Green**. *(1½ miles)*

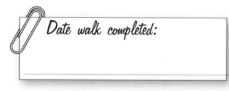

*Date walk completed:*

# WESTCOTT, BROADMOOR, LEITH HILL AND COLDHARBOUR

**THE 17TH CENTURY PLOUGH INN HAS THE DISTINCTION OF BEING IN SURREY'S HIGHEST VILLAGE AND ALSO HAS ITS OWN BREWERY**

**Distance:**
8$^1/_4$ miles

**Starting point:**
Holy Trinity church,
Westcott.
GR: 139484

**Map:** OS Landranger 187 Dorking & Reigate, Crawley & Horsham

**How to get there:** *Westcott is 1 mile west of Dorking on the A25. Holy Trinity church is at the western end on a knoll near the village green. The church parking area can be used at most times except Sunday morning. Alternatively, there is plenty of parking around the village.*

*T*his magnificent circuit leads you along a pleasant track that follows a valley floor where the adjacent fields contain a string of ponds and a woodland waterfall is passed. After passing through the hamlet of Broadmoor it continues on a wide path flanked by mature stands of pine that exude their invigorating scent on the breeze. The route easily climbs the 700 feet rise required to reach the summit of Leith Hill where you can drink in the far-reaching views over the Surrey landscape.

After passing Leith Hill tower the way descends into the village of Coldharbour and meets the welcoming Plough Inn. From here the direction changes as the circuit heads back to Westcott along an old byway through the forest. Another change of direction leads you down the slopes of Squires Great Wood to farmland with expansive views. After passing attractive cottages, the route returns to Westcott and the end of this great walk.

Under the crest of Leith Hill lies the quiet village of Coldharbour, Surrey's highest and a Mecca for walkers. The **Plough Inn** has something to offer all tastes, especially those that appreciate good real ale, as the pub brews its own. The Leith Hill Brewery was established here in 1996 and produces traditional ales that include Crooked Furrow and Tallywhacker, both exclusive to the pub. Other beers served are Ringwood Old Thumper, Shepherd Neame Spitfire and ever changing guest ales.

As well as ploughman's lunches, there are lunchtime meals such as large pork and leek sausage with mashed potato and onion gravy while the evening menu brings chargrilled lamb steak with red wine jus and many other delights.

**Opening times** *are from 11.30 am to 11 pm on Monday to Saturday and 12 noon to 10.30 pm on Sunday. Food is served each lunchtime and evening and although booking is preferred it is not essential. Telephone: 01306 711793.*

 *The Walk*

① From **Holy Trinity church**, go uphill along the lane and at the top of the rise turn right on a grassy path that remains parallel to a few houses. When the path and lane converge, carry on along a drive opposite and, when the drive ends in 30 yards, press on ahead on a

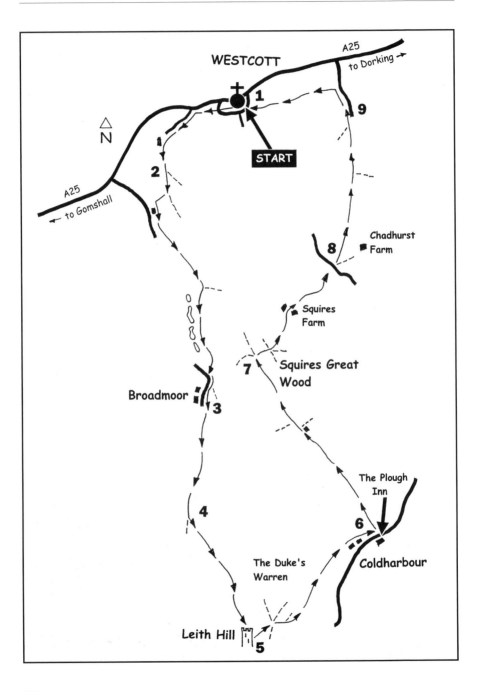

path signposted **GW** (Greensand Way long distance path). At the end of the path, by a house named **Rookery Lodge**, turn left along **Rookery Lane**. Soon after passing a large barn, go right with the lane where you pass a cascade of water at the end of a millpond, the site of **Rookery Mill**. At the gates of a small housing complex named **The Rookery**, turn left on a bridleway. (³/₄ mile)

*These houses are built on the site of a house named The Rookery, where in 1766 Thomas Malthus,* *clergyman, economist and the prophet of population expansion, was born. He wrote his 'Essay on the Principle of Population' here, in which he argued that mankind would expand faster than food production and without some sort of birth control we were all doomed.*

② Continue along the bridleway and bear right over a stile marked **GW**, pressing on uphill on a narrower path through woodland. Cross a stile at the top of the rise to meet a byway. Ignore a stile ahead

LEITH HILL TOWER IS A FOLLY BUILT BY RICHARD HULL IN 1766 TO RAISE THE HEIGHT OF LEITH HILL TO 1,000 FT ABOVE SEA LEVEL

of you and bear right along the byway. Just 5 yards before it meets a lane, go left on a drive to immediately pass the front of a house. Fork left in 20 yards on a track signed **GW**. Remain on this lovely track as it leads you along a valley floor where later you will pass a woodland waterfall before arriving at riding stables in the hamlet of **Broadmoor.** *(1¹/₂ miles)*

③ Here we leave the **Greensand Way** by passing the stables and continuing ahead along a road that is sprinkled with pretty houses. The lane ends by **Whiteberry Cottage** and you should press on ahead along a rising track through woodland, ignoring paths to left and right. Maintain direction ahead when you meet a broad forestry track. In 130 yards, when the track bends sharply right, go ahead on a wide stony bridleway. At a marker post in a further 130 yards, keep ahead. In 120 yards at a third marker post by a fork in the track, bear left on the stony bridleway. *(³/₄ mile)*

④ When another bridleway joins this from the right, keep ahead. At a distinct fork, bear left on a narrower stony path with exposed tree roots. Now maintain direction ahead along the still rising track to eventually meet the open hillside and **Leith Hill tower.** *(³/₄ mile)*

*Leith Hill is Surrey's highest point at 965 feet above sea level. In 1766 a gentleman named Richard Hull built the tower as a folly in order to raise the height of the hill to over 1,000 feet, and several years later, after his death, he was laid to rest beneath its floor. Later, to stop people carrying away the stonework, the door was bricked up and the lower floor was filled with concrete. In 1864 Mr Evelyn of Wotton, a descendant of John Evelyn the 17th century diarist, added the stair turret you see today and during Victorian times the battlement was added, raising the top of the tower to 1,029 feet above sea level.*

⑤ Continue leftwards past the tower on a wide track that goes downhill to meet a large junction of tracks in a gully. Ignore a path marked **GW** to your left and a path that cuts deeply through the hillside to your right. Our way is to fork right and in 20 yards, at a second fork, you should keep right. After 100 yards go over a crossing track and pass between low posts. Now turn immediately left on a path that remains along the top of the escarpment. Keep ahead and ignore left turns by green arrowed marker posts. The path remains parallel to the edge of the escarpment and later meets a wide track by **Coldharbour's cricket pitch** – surely the highest in Surrey. Now go ahead along the descending track to reach **Coldharbour** and the **Plough** public house. (*3/4 mile*)

⑥ After well-earned refreshment, cross the road and continue along an old byway, named **Wolvens Lane**, opposite the pub. After passing between houses and stabling, the tarmac surface ends and you should continue ahead along a wide track. In 200 yards keep left at a fork and follow this old byway without deviation for 1 mile until a signed bridleway crossing track is reached. (*1 1/4 miles*)

⑦ Leave the byway now and turn right on the bridleway. In 120 yards ignore a side path and continue down the eroded track to meet a junction of tracks in 50 yards. Now, make sure you choose the correct path. Ignore tracks to left and right and the one ahead of you. The way is to fork left on a narrower stony downhill path. Soon at a fork keep to the left and continue on a downhill path that brings you to gentrified **Squires Farm**. Turn right, passing the house, and continue

along the driveway until it ends at a road. (*3/4 mile*)

⑧ Cross a stile opposite and go diagonally left over a field to reach and cross a stile in the bottom left corner. Press on along a well-defined path until another field is reached, which you enter. Follow the left-hand field edge to meet a stile beside a gate. Ignore a footpath on your immediate right and continue ahead along the fenced path until a road is met by **Keeper's Cottage**. (*1 mile*)

⑨ The way continues along this pleasing road where you pass pretty cottages and amusingly eccentric clipped hedges. Look out for a signed **GW** path over a small bridge to your left, which you should follow. When you reach a cluster of houses, continue along the path to the right of a bungalow named **Luck Hollow**. Soon, at a driveway, continue ahead on the **GW** path that brings you to a road alongside a churchyard. Here turn right and retrace your steps the short distance back to **Holy Trinity church**. (*3/4 mile*)

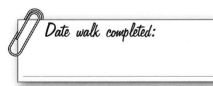

*Date walk completed:*

# RANMORE, FETCHAM DOWNS AND MICKLEHAM

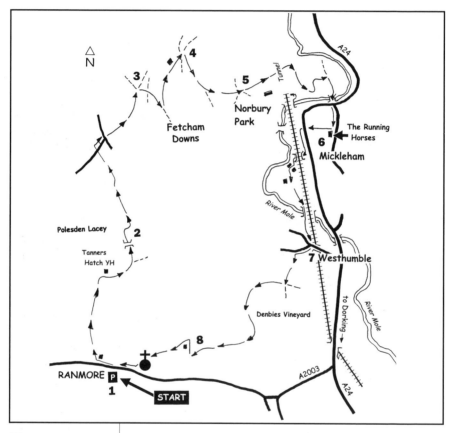

| Distance: | Map: OS Landranger 187 Dorking & Reigate, Crawley & Horsham |
|---|---|
| 10$^{1}/_{2}$ miles | |
| **Starting point:** The National Trust pay and display car park on Ranmore Common. GR: 142503 | **How to get there:** *From the A24 by Dorking Station go west along Ashcombe Road (A2003). Continue ahead at a mini roundabout and then turn right into Ranmore Road. The car park is to the left at the crest of the hill.* |

THE VIEW ACROSS THE VALE OF MICKLEHAM AS THE TRACK DESCENDS FROM NORBURY PARK

*T*his undulating circuit begins on top of the North Downs and heads away from the escarpment on a scenic cart track through magnificent woodland. After circumnavigating the parkland of Polesden Lacey – one of Surrey's finest houses – the walk crosses Fetcham Downs, with far-reaching views, and continues through the peaceful woodland of Norbury Park. Here the way joins a driveway that will lead you down into the Vale of Mickleham where, after crossing the River Mole, you come to the superb Running Horses pub and restaurant in the village of Mickleham.

After leaving the pub, the route re-crosses the river and continues through fields to reach Westhumble. Not far from here the North Downs Way long distance path begins a fairly energetic ascent through Denbies Wine Estate, the largest in Britain. As you gain height on your way back to Ranmore Common, the views over the vineyard are quite spectacular and worth the effort of the climb.

The village of Mickleham is nowadays fortunately bypassed by the busy A24 and a stroll along its single street is a pleasure. Near the Norman church there is a fine selection of buildings, including The Old House of 1636 and nearby Burmester House of the 18th century. Opposite the church is the **Running Horses** inn and restaurant – said to originate from the 16th century although it is much restored and altered. The mouthwatering food is freshly prepared to order and ranges from a substantial chip butty on the bar menu to a mushroom and spinach soufflé dish, served with blue cheese sauce, on the main menu. The choice of beers is pretty wide and includes Fuller's London Pride, Young's Best, King & Barnes Sussex, Friary Meaux Best, Morland Old Speckled Hen and a changing guest beer.

**Opening times** *are from 11.30 am to 3 pm and 5.30 pm to 11 pm on Monday to Saturday and 12 noon to 3.30 pm and 7 pm to 10.30 pm on Sunday. Cooked food is available from 12 noon to 2.30 pm and from 7 pm to 9.30 pm, except Sunday evening. Booking in the restaurant is essential on Friday, Saturday and Sunday. Telephone: 01372 372279.*

① From the car park, cross the road and turn left along a wide grassy strip. In 180 yards pass **Fox Cottage** on your right and turn right on a cart track signposted to a youth hostel. Keep to this track as it leads you through magnificent woodland. Remain on the track at a bend and pass the remote **Tanners Hatch Youth Hostel**. Ignore a right turn and stay on the main track as it descends to the valley floor. Soon ignore a right fork and keep ahead to quite unexpectedly pass under an ornate bridge. *(1½ miles)*

② Now keep ahead and continue following the track up the other side of the valley until it finally meets a road. Cross the road and turn immediately right along an avenue of beech trees to reach a small road junction. Here maintain direction along an old byway between fields to a junction of tracks. *(1¾ miles)*

③ Turn right at this junction and soon pass through a line of trees. Keep ahead on a path that skirts a field to your left with woodland on your right. When the field ends, ignore a path ahead and turn hard left to continue alongside the field, again with woodland to your right. Pass by the unusually named **Roaringhouse Farm** and continue to a junction of tracks in 180 yards. *(1 mile)*

④ Now ignore a narrow path on your immediate right but turn right on a wide stony track signed as a bridleway. This is **Norbury Park**, a beautiful area that is now in the capable hands of the **Surrey Wildlife Trust**. At a fork, bear left on a track through a pretty wildflower meadow. Continue through trees at the far side and at another fork, with a sawmill to your right, fork left to reach a tarmac drive. (³/₄ mile)

⑤ Now go ahead along the drive and soon pass the entranceway to **Norbury Park House**. Remain on the drive as it zigzags down into the **Vale of Mickleham**. Along the way look out for a galvanised steel fence, designed and built in 2002 by

Terrence Clark, a local craftsman, and admire his artistically designed seats that form an integral part of the fence – so much more civilised than barbed wire, don't you think?

*Norbury Park is named after Sir Henry Norbury, who owned the estate in the mid 15th century. Surrey Wildlife Trust now manages the 1,300 acres of wooded parkland and three tenanted farms on behalf of Surrey County Council. The scenery wasn't always like this, though, as the downland hilltop was without trees until the mid 18th century when George Lock bought the estate and created woodland walks and plantations. On Bowen's map of 1760 the area is engraved with*

**THE RUNNING HORSES PUB AND RESTAURANT IN MICKLEHAM**

*the words 'Norbury is remarkable for its Orchard, in which tis said are contained upwards of 40 thousand Walnut Trees'. Although the sheep walks have been replaced with woodland, the area is quite outstanding.*

The drive finally ends at a T-junction. Turn right along a lane and cross the **River Mole** to meet the A24 dual carriageway. Cross the road and continue ahead along **Old London Road** to reach the **Running Horses** pub and restaurant. (1½ miles)

⑥ From the pub the route continues along **Swanworth Lane**, which runs alongside the premises. Proceed ahead and soon you will reach the A24. Cross to the far side and continue along **Swanworth Lane**. Keep left at a fork and continue past the gateway to a house named **Travellers Rest**. Pass under a railway bridge and soon the lane ends by farm buildings and a junction of tracks. Turn left here along a fenced cart track and when this soon ends by a house continue through a kissing gate. Press on across a field on a well-worn path, parallel to a railway line. Cross a bridge over the **River Mole** and continue along the left side of a field to reach a fenced path where you continue ahead to meet a road junction at **Westhumble**. (1½ miles)

⑦ The way now continues rightwards along **Chapel Lane**. Some 20 yards after passing the end of a private road named **Pilgrims Way**, turn left on a narrow fenced public footpath between gardens. When this ends, pass through two kissing gates to reach a well-worn crossing track signed as the **North Downs Way.** Turn right along this track and keep to it at all times. As it climbs up the **North Downs** it passes through **Denbies Vineyard** where the views from the open hillside are outstanding. After leaving the vineyard, the track levels out and meets a junction of paths. *(1¾ miles)*

⑧ Turn right and continue following the **North Downs Way**. Soon after passing a white cottage, turn left along the signposted path and at a road maintain direction ahead alongside it to pass **St Barnabas' church** and the former school. Ahead is a road junction where by turning right you will see the car park and the end of this superb walk. **Steers Field** by the car park has lovely views over **Dorking** and makes a perfect picnic spot. *(¾ mile)*

*Date walk completed:*

86

# BROCKHAM, PARKGATE AND GADBROOK

**THE SURREY OAKS, AT PARKGATE, IS A POPULAR REAL ALE PUB**

**Distance:**
12 miles

**Starting point:**
Beside the church
on the southern
edge of Brockham
village green.
GR: 197495

**Map:** OS Landranger 187 Dorking & Reigate, Crawley & Horsham

**How to get there:** *Brockham lies 1¹/₂ miles east of
Dorking, off the A25. Park beside the church in Wheelers
Lane.*

*W*onderful field paths are a feature of this circuit – and the number of watering holes along the way. Starting off by Brockham's lovely village green, the route heads south-west to meet the Royal Oak at Stonebridge before turning south and making its way past Blackbrook on scenic paths with extensive views towards Leith Hill. Later a lovely farm track leads you past exceptional old houses before bringing you to Parkgate and the joys of the welcoming Surrey Oaks pub. After leaving Parkgate the way passes between the trees of Hammond's Copse where the woodland floor is suffused in wildflowers during early May. More super field paths lead you towards Dawesgreen, where you may wish to divert a few yards to the 17th century Seven Stars pub for refreshment. After passing through Gadbrook the route brings you to the parkland above the River Mole at Betchworth, where there are more outstanding views, before finally ending back at Brockham.

In a quiet corner of the county lies a hamlet that has the good fortune of being the home of one of Surrey's finest pubs, the wonderful **Surrey Oaks** at Parkgate. Parts of the building date back to the late 16th century but it wasn't until 1850 that it became an inn. In recent years it has been voted CAMRA pub of the year several times and it is no wonder why – real ale drinkers will be enthralled by the choice of ales that include Adnam's Southwold, Harvey's Sussex Best and two constantly changing guests from 'micro' breweries. The food is delicious and ranges from baguettes and ploughman's to hot dishes such as steak and kidney pudding and deep fried whole scampi tails. Look out for the 'daily specials' posted on the blackboard.

*Opening times are from 11.30 am to 2.30 pm and 5.30 pm to 11 pm on Monday to Friday, 11.30 am to 3 pm and 6 pm to 11 pm on Saturday and 12 noon to 3 pm and 7 pm to 10.30 pm on Sunday. Hot food is available during lunchtimes and evenings, except on Sunday evening. Booking for the restaurant at weekends is advisable. Telephone: 01306 631200.*

## The Walk

The name Brockham is derived from 'broc' or brook and refers to

the Tanner's Brook that joins the River Mole here.

① From **Wheelers Lane**, go to the village green and continue along the

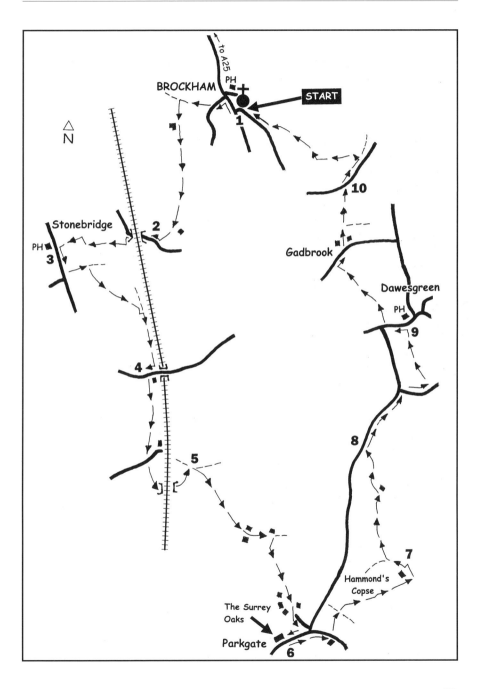

left-hand pavement where you pass **Brockham Village Hall**. Soon pass pretty cottages and go left along **Old School Lane**. Bear right on a rough track immediately after passing over **Tanner's Brook**. By trees to your left, go left over a stile and continue along the right-hand side of a field to pass **Pondtail Farm**. Continue along the right side of several more fields to meet a farm track to the rear of a house on your left. Press on to reach another field and follow the left side beside **Tanner's Brook** to soon cross a stile to join a lane. *(1¹/₂ miles)*

② Turn right along the lane and then left along **Scammells Farm** drive after going under a railway bridge. In 30 yards turn right and cross a stile in a hedgerow. Now continue ahead along the right-hand field edge to meet a second field, where you maintain direction. Cross a wooden bridge and skirt the next field rightwards to finally meet a road by the charming **Royal Oak** pub at **Stonebridge**. *(³/₄ mile)*

③ Go left alongside the road and when near the crest of a low rise, turn left on a signed footpath along a gated farm track. Pass through a second gate by power cables and, ignoring a gate ahead, turn right and soon pass through a gate in a field edge. Go under power cables and cross the field towards a large oak tree ahead, where you cross a

stile. Continue along the left side of the next field and cross a stile in the corner, maintaining direction to reach a field gate. Pass through the gate and keep to the right-hand side of the next field to meet and cross a stile in the far corner. Now skirt the edge of the field leftwards before turning right on a path that remains parallel to a railway line. Continue along the edge of fields to reach a road. *(1¹/₄ miles)*

④ Turn right along the road for 100 yards before turning left on a bridleway through woodland to meet a field gate. Go through this and maintain direction ahead through a couple of fields to reach a cart track. At a junction of tracks by **Lodge Farm**, press on ahead along a concrete drive and pass under a railway bridge. Remain on the curving drive until it ends at a T-junction. *(1¹/₄ miles)*

⑤ Turn right here along the track and soon ignore a left fork. After leading you through woodland, the track continues alongside **Ewood Old Farmhouse** and **Mill Cottage**, both timber framed and ancient. Keep ahead and after passing a couple of Victorian cottages to your left, go right over a stile. Continue across a grassy area and, just before reaching a field, turn left on a narrow path through scrub. Ignore side paths to meet a group of modern executive houses. At a gate fork left on a narrow path, where you should soon ignore a right turn. Keep ahead alongside a garden and go through a gate to reach a driveway. Turn right along the drive and pass the end of a road named **Becket Wood** to reach a T-junction. Turn right along the road and within yards turn right again at a road junction by **Partridge Lane** to reach the **Surrey Oaks** pub within yards. *(1³/₄ miles)*

⑥ After suitable refreshment, retrace your steps to the road junction and continue along **Partridge Lane**. When opposite the second house on your right, cross a stile to your left and continue ahead to reach **Hammond's Copse**. Now follow the well-defined path through trees and keep ahead at a crossing path. Go ahead at a junction of tracks and a further crossing path to finally reach a stile at a field edge. Press on over the centre of this field and cross a

stile 80 yards to the right of farm buildings and cross another in 15 yards. Here the path divides and our way is diagonally left across a corner of a field, which you should exit via a field gate. Turn left for a few yards on a drive before going right by the gates of **Parkhouse Farm**. *(1 mile)*

⑦ The path brings you to a gate at the edge of **Hammond's Copse**. Do not go through the gate but fork right on a path that remains parallel to a field. Soon cross two stiles in quick succession and press on along the left side of a large field. Go over a stile in the corner and another in 10 yards. Now go diagonally right and cross a small concrete bridge to enter another field. Cross the field to a stile 100 yards to the left of a house at **Brook Farm**. Continue over a farm drive and a stile. In 10 yards cross two stiles in quick succession on your left before

**BROCKHAM VILLAGE GREEN NESTLES BELOW THE SOUTHERN FLANK OF THE NORTH DOWNS**

bearing right along a field edge. At the crest of a rise, enter a second field and go diagonally right to reach a stile in the corner. Press on through a small coppice to meet a road. *(1 mile)*

⑧ Turn right along the road and then right into **Clayhill Road**. Soon after rounding a bend, go left over a stile and continue alongside a large field, with woodland on your left. At the end of the woodland, follow the field edge leftwards before continuing right and regaining your original direction. Cross a stile at the end of the field and continue along a fenced path to meet a road. If thirst is overtaking you, a detour of 100 yards to the right brings you to the **Seven Stars**, another fine country pub. *(1 mile)*

⑨ The route continues leftwards along the road where it passes **Leigh Village Hall**. Ignore a footpath on your left, but 120 yards later turn right over a stile on a signed footpath. Keep ahead through the centre of a field and cross a stile at the far side. Now go diagonally left across the next field to meet a marker post by an oak tree. Press on ahead now and at the

end of this field cross a couple of stiles and brooks. Keep ahead and cross a further stile to finally reach a road. Ignore a footpath ahead of you and turn right along the road. When the road bends to the right in the hamlet of **Gadbrook**, turn left on a rough track by a wall-mounted postbox and continue between a couple of houses to reach a field. Go directly ahead over this and a second field to reach a road. *(1¼ miles)*

⑩ Turn right alongside the road and in 120 yards cross a stile on your left. Remain roughly parallel with the road until, opposite another stile on your right, you turn left to meet the edge of woodland. Here turn left again and follow a well-defined path along a row of oak trees lining the brow of a hill above the **River Mole**. Cross a stile and continue ahead alongside woodland and, at its end, turn right along its edge to reach and cross a stile. Now go diagonally left to a stile in the corner of the field and continue along a path to reach **Wheelers Lane**. Turn right along the road and after passing the village school, you reach the church and the end of this super circuit. *(1¼ miles)*

*Date walk completed:*

# EPSOM DOWNS, GREAT HURST WOOD AND HEADLEY

**THE VIEW FROM WALTON DOWNS, WITH THE STEEPLE OF HEADLEY CHURCH IN THE DISTANCE**

**Distance:**
7¹/₂ miles

**Starting point:**
Tattenham Corner.
GR: 224585

**Map:** OS Landranger 187 Dorking & Reigate, Crawley & Horsham

**How to get there:** *Tattenham Corner on Epsom Downs is off the B290 between Epsom and Tadworth. There are parking areas on both sides of the road.*

*T*hose that enjoy horse racing will need no introduction to Epsom Downs, but have you been there and walked the elevated downs, or admired the extensive views over London from their breezy heights? Well, this enjoyable shorter walk will introduce you to the lovely area where the rolling downs meet the fields and woodland of Headley to the south. Beginning by the famous Tattenham Corner bend, the route crosses Epsom Downs before descending Walton Downs and meeting easy-to-follow paths that take you to Headley.

For most of the outward route you will see Headley's church spire above the treeline and before long the church is reached and a few yards further brings you to the Cock Horse and welcome refreshment. From here the way soon joins a lovely track that returns you to Walton Downs. More easy tracks bring you to Epsom Downs where the walk passes close to the grandstands before ending at Tattenham Corner. The downs are shut on the few race days in the year.

 Other than the small group of cottages that separate the pub from the church on the crest of a hill, the spread-out village of Headley doesn't really have a centre. For as long as I can remember, the pub was called the Cock, but more recently a horse has appeared in the name, making it the **Cock Horse**. There are views over the fields from the pleasant garden where you may wish to sit at a table in the summer and consume one of the snacks, which include baguettes and burgers. For something more substantial, why not try the Thai vegetable curry or an 8 oz rump steak? The pumps deliver Worthington's Best, Fuller's London Pride, Morland Old Speckled Hen and a beer called Black Sheep.

**Opening times** *are from 12 noon to 11.20 pm each day (Sunday closing is at 10.50 pm). Cooked food is available from 12 noon to 2 pm and 6 pm to 8 pm on Monday to Friday and from 12 noon to 4 pm and 6 pm to 8.30 pm at weekends (not Sunday evening). Booking is necessary for larger parties. Telephone: 01372 377258.*

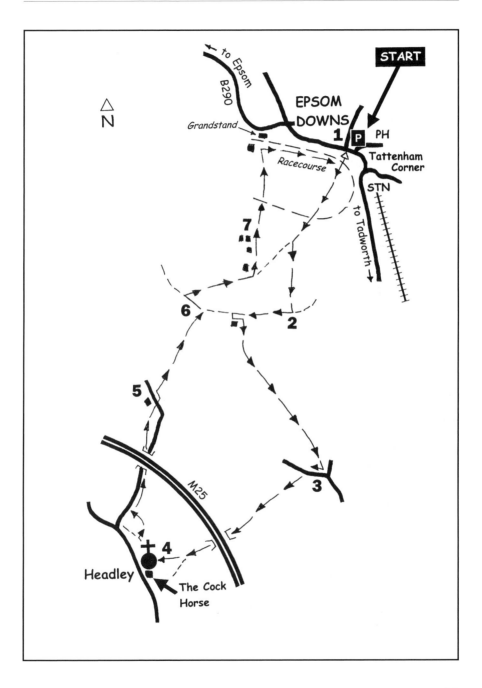

# The Walk

Epsom first became famous for its wells and reviving waters and at one time rivalled Bath as a spa town. A second rise to fame came when, as Lord Rosebery, a 19th century Prime Minister and inhabitant of Epsom, famously described it: 'Though the waters failed us, a miracle yet remained to be wrought on Epsom. In the last quarter of the 18th century a roistering party at a neighbouring country-house founded two races, in two successive years, one for 3-year old colts and fillies, the other for 3-year old fillies, and named them gratefully after their host and his house – the Derby and the Oaks. Seldom has a carouse had a more permanent effect.' Having started in 1779, the races are still the most famous in the world and more money changes hands over the Derby than any other race.

① From either parking area, cross the racecourse and continue on a track that bisects this part of the downs. Go over the racecourse at the far side and continue ahead beside woodland on your left. When the woodland ends, bear left on a distinct path that descends **Walton Downs** to meet an all-weather horse track at the foot of the slope. *(1 mile)*

② Cross the track and turn right along a bridleway, with scrub on your left. At a junction of tracks, go left and in 15 yards turn left again to pass the gate of isolated **Nohome Farm**. Turn right here on a narrow stony path, which you should now follow without deviation until you meet a driveway. Press on ahead along the drive to soon reach a road. *(1¹/₄ miles)*

③ Turn right along the road and when it bends to the right, bear left on a bridleway. Keep to this bridleway and eventually pass under the M25. Keep ahead and as the motorway noise recedes you will reach the sanctuary of **Great Hurst Wood**, where during springtime the woodland floor is carpeted by bluebells. Bear right when the path divides and soon press on through a kissing gate to reach the graveyard of **St Mary's church**. Ignore paths to left and right and continue through the graveyard to meet a short lane where you will find the **Cock Horse** with the very attractive **Old School House** opposite. *(1¹/₄ miles)*

*As you enter the graveyard you will immediately pass to the left of a well-preserved wooden grave board, once a common sight in Surrey churchyards. A little further along the path is a strange flint grotto that forms the burial vault of a local family. The original*

96

*church fell into such disrepair that it was knocked down and rebuilt in 1850. This vault is made from the rubble from the medieval church that once occupied this site.*

④ After refreshment, return to the graveyard and pass through the kissing gate. Turn left on a fenced path that on clear days offers views over **London** and as far as **Docklands**. At a junction of paths, turn right and continue along a path that during spring is lined by yellow archangel, the old herbal remedy for

sore throats and ulcers. When a road is reached, turn right along it and pass a group of houses. Go under the M25 and in 15 yards cross a stile on your left. Some 80 yards later, go right over a stile and cross a small paddock. Continue ahead on a fenced path between fields with wonderful spreading chestnut trees. The path finally ends at a road by a house. *(1 mile)*

⑤ Turn left along the road for a few yards and then go right on a wide track opposite the house. Follow this very pleasant downhill track now as

ONCE KNOWN AS THE COCK, THE PUB HAS MORE LATTERLY ACQUIRED A HORSE IN ITS NAME

it leads you to the foot of **Walton Downs** where it ends at a T-junction with a wide farm track. *(1 mile)*

⑥ Continue leftwards along the farm track, ignoring a right fork. At a left bend in the track, with fields ahead of you, turn right on a rising stony path between trees. Keep ahead at a crossing track and continue on a tarmac drive with a hedgerow on your left. Remain on this drive as it passes through woodland and turns sharply left. Continue ahead at a crossing track and pass a lonely house. Maintain direction along the main track and ignore a couple of right forks as it passes the end of residential roads. *(1 mile)*

⑦ Keep ahead when the path narrows and go over an all-weather track for horses. Cross open downs before continuing alongside scrub to your left to reach the racecourse. Go left alongside the rails and in 10 yards cross the racecourse. Press on over a tarmac drive and continue on a distinct path that will bring you to a parking area to the left of the

grandstands. Here ignore a drive on your immediate right, but go right along a hard surfaced track that remains parallel to the racecourse and passes the front of the stands. Keep to this track until, after passing the 3-furlong marker, you turn left to re-cross the racecourse at **Tattenham Corner** where this lovely circuit ends. *(1 mile)*

*Tattenham Corner was of course the place where Emily Davison threw herself under the hooves of the King's horse during the 1913 Derby, thereby attracting attention to the cause of the Suffragettes, to which she was dedicated. She had previously suffered the agony of force-feeding by the prison authorities on over 40 occasions. She died of her injuries in Epsom Cottage Hospital on 8th June 1913.*

You will find simple refreshment during daylight hours at **The Downs Lunch Box** café in the car park or for something more substantial the **Tattenham Corner** pub and restaurant is just a few yards away.

Date walk completed:

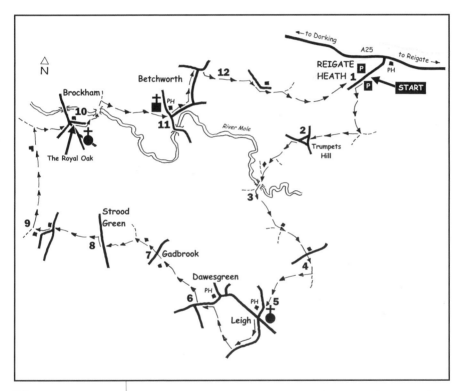

# Walk 16

# REIGATE HEATH, LEIGH, BROCKHAM AND BETCHWORTH

| **Distance:** | **Map:** OS Landranger 187 Dorking & Reigate, Crawley & Horsham |
|---|---|
| 11 miles | |
| **Starting point:** | **How to get there:** *Flanchford Road is ³/₄ mile west of* |
| *The parking area in* | *Reigate, off the A25. Turn southwards off the A25 by a* |
| *Flanchford Road.* | *cricket pitch to reach the parking area in ¹/₄ mile.* |
| *GR: 239503* | |

THE WELCOMING ROYAL OAK OCCUPIES AN ENVIABLE POSITION ALONGSIDE BROCKHAM'S PICTURESQUE VILLAGE GREEN

*T*his exhilarating walk through a part of the Weald is superb at any time of the year and you will find plenty of pubs along the route where you can quench your thirst and rest awhile. Starting off on the sandy soils of Reigate Heath, the circuit follows appealing paths across fields with panoramic views and brings you to Leigh – pronounced Lye. Here the route passes the picturesque village green with church, pub and ancient Priests' House before continuing over more splendid field paths, with outstanding views towards the slopes of Box Hill.

As the route passes by the side of Strood Green, it follows a lovely path over fields to bring you to the Royal Oak public house beside Brockham's pretty village green. Leaving here, the circuit crosses the River Mole and follows a section of the Greensand Way long distance path through the southern end of Betchworth before rejoining Reigate Heath.

With the slopes of Box Hill acting as its backdrop, the **Royal Oak** enjoys an enviable position alongside the much-photographed village green at Brockham, which still retains its pump. Tables at the front of the pub offer the chance of watching village life go by, while to the rear there is a pleasant garden. I enjoyed a filling ploughman's lunch whilst sitting in the shade of a gaily-coloured umbrella on my summertime walk, but you might well choose one of the satisfying cooked meals from the ever-changing menu. Alternatively, look out for the 'daily specials' advertised on the blackboard as they are always good value and will not disappoint.

The beers are kept well and include Harvey's Sussex, Fuller's London Pride and Wadworth 6X, plus the usual lagers and stouts. This is a popular pub, which makes booking a table necessary if you wish to opt for a full meal here.

**Opening times** *are from 11 am to 3 pm and 5.50 pm to 11 pm on weekdays, 11 am to 11 pm on Saturday and 12 noon to 10.30 pm on Sunday. Cooked food is available every lunchtime and evening, except Sunday evening. Telephone: 01737 843241.*

 *The Walk*

① From the parking area, continue west along the **Flanchford Road** and turn left along **Bonnys Road**. Ignore a left fork by cottages, but 20 yards later fork left along a bridleway that passes the side of the **Skimington Castle** pub. The path passes through woodland to reach a junction of paths by a driveway where you should turn right over a stile and press on along a fenced footpath to eventually meet a road junction. *(1¹/₄ miles)*

② Cross the road and continue along **Trumpets Hill Road**. Soon bear left on the drive to **Little**

**Santon Farm** and in 25 yards bear left again on a fenced footpath. Maintain direction ahead over three stiles to reach a junction of tracks. Go ahead along a bridleway and pass the house and buildings of **Ricebridge Farm**. Ignore a stile on your right and carry on along the bridleway to meet and cross a bridge over the **River Mole**. *(³/₄ mile)*

③ Bear left here up a slope to reach a field. Continue along the left-hand field edge and when the boundary goes left you should maintain direction ahead to cross a small tributary of the main river. Fork half right and pass by an oak tree before continuing ahead across a field to reach a marker post by a stile. Cross the stile and now go diagonally left through a field with a byre to your left. Ignore a stile opposite this structure and press on ahead along the right-hand field edge. Keep ahead, crossing two further stiles, to pass through a ribbon of woodland. Press on over a stile and continue along a path to the right of a house to reach a road. (3/4 mile)

④ Continue on a footpath opposite and cross a small bridge over a stream to reach and cross a stile. Now turn immediately right along the field edge and within yards go right over a stile and re-cross the stream. Follow a waymarked path along the right edge of three fields. At a fourth field, go diagonally left to meet a kissing gate in the top corner. (3/4 mile)

⑤ Go through the kissing gate and continue leftwards along a road to meet the village green at **Leigh** where, behind a fence to your left, there is the 15th century **Priests' House**. Pass by the **Plough** pub to meet crossroads where the way continues ahead along **Clayhill**

ST BARTHOLOMEW'S CHURCH IN LEIGH

Road. After passing the entrance to Clayhill Farm, turn right on a signed footpath where you continue along the left side of a large field with woodland on your left. Follow the field edge at the end of the woodland and at a corner turn right along its edge to regain your original direction. Go over a stile in the top corner and continue on a path to reach a road. *(1 mile)*

⑥ Turn left alongside the road; then, 30 yards before a road junction, turn right over a stile and cross the centre of a large field. Ahead you will see the **North Downs**, displaying the white scar of the **Betchworth Chalk Quarry**. Enter a second field and cross to a marker post under an oak tree in the left corner. Go ahead along the left side of the next field to a stile. Continue along a fenced path and cross the **Gad Brook** to soon pass an avenue of poplars to meet a road. *(³/₄ mile)*

*Along the North Downs there are many chalk quarries where for centuries the chalk was processed in limekilns and used to improve the sour greensand soils. The chalk face at Betchworth, once over 200 feet high, has almost disappeared under a landfill site and quite surprisingly this is now a Site of Special Scientific Interest. Surrey Wildlife Trust, who benefit through the landfill tax, are advising on the restoration of the flora and fauna. The Trust has also converted an old limekiln at Brockham Quarry into a successful bat hibernaculum.*

⑦ Cross the road and continue ahead along a wide track to reach a junction of paths by the front garden of a house. Bear left here and ignore a stile on your immediate left. Continue on a path alongside a garage and garden to soon meet a field. Go ahead along the field edge to a second stile where the path now divides. Turn left here and remain along the edge of woodland. Maintain direction along the waymarked path until a road is met. *(¹/₂ mile)*

⑧ Turn right alongside the road and then turn left into **Tweed Lane**. Continue ahead at a junction to soon meet the end of the road. Keep straight on now along a broad byway to reach a country lane by **Bushbury Farm**. Turn left to a small road junction and then go right along a lane and pass the farm buildings. Just before the lane bends to the left, bear right through a farm gate and continue ahead to go over **Tanner's Brook** and meet a crossing path. *(³/₄ mile)*

⑨ The way is rightwards over a stile and you now follow the left edge of several fields. After crossing two farm tracks, the second of which is by **Pondtail Farm**, the path ends at a wide crossing track. Here we meet the **Greensand Way** long distance path, which we are to follow to the end of the walk. Turn right along the broad track and at a road go left to reach the pretty village green in **Brockham**. Go ahead and pass the village pump to meet the **Royal Oak** public house. *(1¹/₄ miles)*

⑩ The circuit continues on past the pub to where the lane ends by the village pound. Turn left here on a tarmac path that leads you over the **River Mole** where you press on up a wide track to a junction of paths. Now turn right on a path that initially passes the rear of gardens. Follow this well-worn path alongside fields and past farm buildings until you reach the churchyard in **Betchworth**. Continue alongside the church to meet a road by the **Dolphin** public house. *(1 mile)*

⑪ Go ahead along **Wonham Lane** and bear left on a signposted path alongside a field edge to meet a road named **Sandy Lane**. Turn left along the road and at a T-junction turn right. In 20 yards turn right on a path between cottages and climb steep steps. Cross a stile and continue along a field edge to a second stile. Go over this and bear diagonally left to a stile in the far left corner of the field by a bridleway. *(³/₄ mile)*

⑫ Turn right on the bridleway for 5 yards and then go left and continue along the **Greensand Way**. The path crosses fields and passes close to a house to meet a farm lane. Turn right along the lane to pass between the buildings of **Dungate's Farm** and maintain direction ahead along a wide track. Soon the track divides and our way is ahead through a field gate on a track that ends beside a house and a golf club fairway. Go over the fairway to a well-used track opposite and now follow it as it shadows **Flanchford Road** and finally brings you to the parking area and the end of this enjoyable walk. *(1¹/₂ miles)*

*Date walk completed:*

# CHARLWOOD, NEWDIGATE AND CAPEL

**THE CROWN INN AT CAPEL IS A GEM; EVEN THE VINE AT THE FRONT OF THE BUILDING HAS A PRESERVATION ORDER ON IT!**

**Distance:** 10³/₄ miles

**Map:** OS Landranger 187 Dorking & Reigate, Crawley & Horsham

**Starting point:** The village green in The Street, Charlwood. GR: 244410

**How to get there:** *Charlwood is 3 miles west of the A217 at Horley. The Street runs east-west through the village.*

*T*his captivating circuit starts in an area under threat from the enlargement of Gatwick Airport and, although much of the way is under the flight path, the countryside is outstanding and not to be missed. After following field paths, the route meets a quiet unmade road that leads you past a moated manor house at Cudworth and brings you to Newdigate by its wood-shingled church and the superb Six Bells pub. More field paths are followed to reach Capel, where the way continues along its main street to meet up with the Crown Inn and the halfway mark of the walk.

After leaving the glories of the Crown, the circuit continues across scenic fields before returning to Charlwood through Glover's Wood, an outstanding area of woodland untouched since Saxon times. Come here during early summer and be treated to displays of wildflowers in sunlit glades while common spotted orchids edge the path.

 Capel once stood on the London to Worthing road and in earlier times the village was an important staging post. The gently curving main street is a happy mix of houses young and old that gel well together. Occupying a prominent site next to St John the Baptist church is the 17th century **Crown Inn**. This has seen many changes over the last few centuries, but surely the most important was the modern day bypassing of the village by the A24 coast road. Step inside this atmospheric inn and sample the ever-changing and well-kept real ales. To stifle your hunger pains there is a good range of snacks and meals, ranging from baguettes and salads to more substantial main courses that include a Thai-style crab and coconut fish cakes dish with fresh lime and ginger dressing. There is a very pleasant sitting-out area to the side.

**Opening times** *are from 12 noon to 2.30 pm and 4.30 pm to 11 pm on Monday to Friday, 11 am to 11 pm on Saturday and 12 noon to 10.30 pm on Sunday. Cooked food is available from 12 noon to 2 pm and 6 pm to 9.30 pm (Sunday 12 noon to 4 pm only). Booking is advisable but not always necessary. Telephone: 01306 711130.*

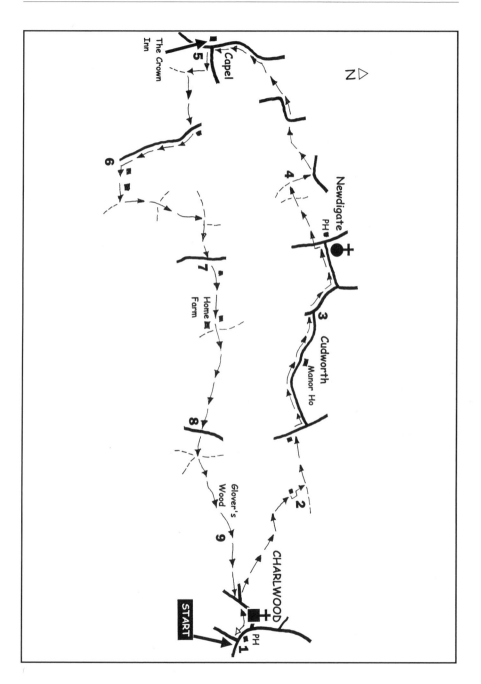

# The Walk

① From the village green, walk along **The Street** and pass the **Rising Sun** pub. In 50 yards fork left along a one-way street and pass the **Half Moon** pub to reach **St Nicholas's church**. Continue through the graveyard and along a path to meet a road. Go ahead along **Glover's Road** and at a slight left bend turn right on a footpath beside a cottage named **Brookside**. Cross a stile to go left alongside its garden and press on to meet another stile. Go over this and bear diagonally right to meet and cross a stile on the edge of woodland and follow the path to reach another field. Press on along its left edge to reach and cross a stile to re-enter woodland. Follow the well-defined path and ignore a left turn. Cross a stile and press on along the left-hand edge of a rising field. Ignore a stile on your left and continue to the top corner. Here turn right and skirt a garden to reach a farm drive by cottages. *(1¼ miles)*

② Turn left along the drive for 30 yards before turning right over a stile and crossing a field to a stile opposite. Now turn left along a well-trodden track that will bring you to a road. Turn right along the road and in 100 yards turn left into **Burntoak Lane**. Keep to this quiet lane and pass by the ancient tithe barn and moated manor house at **Cudworth**. Maintain direction along the lane to reach its end by the gateway of **Green Lane Farm**. *(1¾ miles)*

③ Go right here along the road to meet a T-junction. Turn left into **Church Lane** to reach **St Peter's church** and the fine **Six Bells** pub beyond. Turn left along **Rusper Road** and pass ancient cottages behind a tall hedge. In 80 yards turn right on a signed path along a field edge. Continue along the right-hand side of a second and third field where in 80 yards you should go right over a stile. Now turn left along the field edge to reach and cross a stile in the corner onto a farm track. *(1 mile)*

④ Turn right along the track to meet a road. Go left along the road for 20 yards before turning left over a stile and entering a field. Now go diagonally right to reach the far corner where you continue through woodland to reach a second field. Go slightly right to meet and cross a stile between two oak trees in a hedgerow. Keep ahead over a paddock to reach a road by the entrance to **Broomells Farm**. Turn left along the road and, when it soon bends sharply left, continue ahead on an indistinct footpath. Soon, at a crossing track, go ahead and over a stile under an oak tree

in 10 yards. Now follow a fenced path between fields. After crossing a brook the path ends at the main street in **Capel**. Here turn left to reach the **Crown Inn** beside **St John the Baptist church**.
*(1¹/₂ miles)*

*The name Capel is derived from the word chapel and the area once formed a part of a Dorking parish named 'cum Capella'. The original church was built during the 13th century and, although heavily restored by the Victorians, its roof timbers, west porch and south and west doors are original.*

⑤ After suitable refreshment, cross the road and continue along **Vicarage Lane** opposite. Look out for a stile on your right when opposite a large and well-proportioned house that is now divided into flats. Cross the stile and continue diagonally left through a field. Pass through a gate in the corner and in 10 yards turn right over a stile behind a farm building. Go ahead along the right edge of a field and at the top corner ignore a stile ahead, instead turning left along

the field edge to meet a stile on your right. Go over this and continue leftwards through scrub to cross a stile under an oak tree. Now go diagonally half right across a field to a stile in the corner and pass through woodland to join another field. Go ahead and cross a stile in front of a house to meet a quiet lane by **Aldhurst Farm**. Turn right and remain on the lane until it ends at the entranceway of a house named **Temple Elfande**. *(1¹/₄ miles)*

⑥ The way continues left along the drive to the house, where you pass by its gates and remain ahead through a field gate. Go forward to a T-junction in 100 yards and turn left on a bridleway, soon passing through a gate to enter a field. Press on ahead on a bridleway that runs along the left edge of this and a

**THE DAPPLED SHADE FROM THE TREES OF GLOVER'S WOOD IS MOST WELCOME ON A HOT SUMMER'S DAY**

further three gated fields. When the far corner of the fourth field is met, ignore a gate on your left and turn right on the signed bridleway along the field edge. Ignore a stile on your left and continue ahead over a brook and through a gate to meet a road. *(1¹/₄ miles)*

⑦ Turn left for 15 yards and enter the drive to **Ockley Lodge**. In 10 yards cross a stile on your right and continue left through a paddock. Pass through a gate and a second paddock to meet a drive. Keep ahead along the drive and after passing farm buildings go through the gate of **Home Farm**. At a right bend, go ahead over a stile by an oak tree. Now maintain direction over the centre of two fields and enter woodland. Press on ahead on the well-trodden path and soon cross a stile to continue along a field edge. The path soon re-enters woodland and crosses a substantial wooden bridge over a stream. Fork left up a slope to reach a field and follow its left edge. Look out for a cart track on your left where you should turn left to enter another field. Turn right now and cross a hidden stile 80 yards to the right of a line of conifer trees to reach a road. *(1¹/₄ miles)*

⑧ Turn right and in 10 yards go left over a stile and continue on a waymarked footpath. Cross a stile and a brook to reach a junction of tracks on the edge of **Glover's Wood**. It is important to make sure you select the right path. Ignore a bridleway to your immediate right and go ahead for 10 yards. Now ignore a footpath ahead of you and bear left. In 8 yards you should fork right on a signed footpath. Keep ahead along this waymarked path as it leads you through this beautiful woodland. *(³/₄ mile)*

*Glover's Wood is ancient woodland that has remained largely untouched since Saxon times and yet the planners of Gatwick airport are prepared to destroy this wonderful place to satisfy the ever-increasing demand to travel by air.*

⑨ Finally go through a kissing gate and leave the woodland behind. Press on ahead and pass between buildings to reach **Glover's Road**, which should be followed to its end. Continue ahead on the tarmac path to reach **St Nicholas's church** and retrace your steps to the village green. *(³/₄ mile)*

*Date walk completed:*

# BLETCHINGLEY AND OUTWOOD

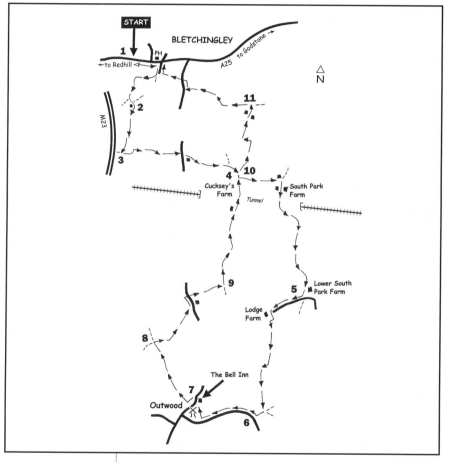

**Distance:**
11 miles

**Map: OS Landranger 187 Dorking & Reigate, Crawley & Horsham**

**Starting point:**
Service road west of
Bletchingley High
Street. GR: 322507

**How to get there:** *Bletchingley straddles the A25
between Redhill and Godstone. The service road is
alongside the A25 and 150 yards west of the Red Lion
pub.*

FINE OLD BUILDINGS OF LOWER SOUTH PARK FARM

*T*his figure-of-eight route is through open farmland, where it follows attractive field paths and cart tracks for most of the way. Beginning by descending easily from Bletchingley's Castle Hill, it continues through fields with scenic views before turning east to join a wonderful farm track that leads to the elegant buildings of South Park Farm. The track continues south, where the elevated views are outstanding, and finally ends at the splendidly kept old buildings of Lower South Park Farm.

Another super track brings you to Outwood where the way passes Outwood Mill and a few yards later reaches the Bell Inn, a good place to take on nourishment. From here the route continues through the pastures of Burstow Park Farm where the views are lovely and the walking is easy. As the way heads north it finally meets the Greensand Way path, which brings you back to Bletchingley and the end of this great walk.

There are two things that attract people to the isolated hamlet of Outwood: the first is the oldest working windmill in England, which stands proudly on the common, and the second is the 17th century **Bell Inn**. While the windmill is open on only a few days during summer, fortunately for us the inn barely closes its doors. It boasts the description *'a little piece of olde England'* and indeed proves this with low ceiling beams from a Charles II man-of-war. The pub has a wide reputation for good food and will not disappoint, whether you order a simple bar snack, homemade soup or one of the more adventurous meals from the à la carte menu in the restaurant. The beers from the pumps include Harvey's Best and Shepherd Neame Spitfire alongside lagers, stout and cider. With open fires in winter and a wonderful garden with fine views, the pub is the perfect spot to rest awhile.

**Opening times** *are from 11 am to 11 pm (Sunday 12 noon to 10.30 pm). Cooked food is available from 12 noon to 2 pm and from 6.30 pm to 9.30 pm (Sunday 12 noon to 9.30 pm). Booking a table is essential if you want to eat in the restaurant. Telephone: 01342 842989.*

## The Walk

① From the service road, walk towards the centre of **Bletchingley** and a few yards after passing the **Red Lion** pub you meet **Stychens Lane**. The way is rightwards across the A25 and along a road named **Castle Square**. When this road soon ends, continue ahead on a path signposted **GW** – the **Greensand Way** long distance path. The path now skirts the mound on which **Bletchingley Castle** was built. Continue on the path as it descends to the fields below and meets a farm track. (*3/4 mile*)

② Ignore a stile ahead of you and bear left along the track to soon meet another. The way is ahead along the **GW** signed path where you pass by the side of a barn. Go over a stile ahead of you and continue along a track that passes through scenic fields marred only slightly by the drone of traffic on the M23 – an ugly scar on such a beautiful landscape. Finally, when the track swings sharply right and is barred by a gate, we leave the **Greensand Way** by pressing on ahead and crossing a stile. (*1/2 mile*)

③ Now turn left along the field edge and cross another stile in the corner. Turn left along the next field edge to the corner and then go rightwards along its left edge. At the far corner, cross another stile and continue alongside a field that skirts a wood. At the end of the woodland, cross a stile on your left and bear right through the next field to meet a stile in the far corner. Go over this and continue along the left side of a field to meet a stile just to the left of a house ahead of you. Cross the stile and small road and continue ahead on a signposted bridleway where you pass **Laundry Cottage**. Press on and later pass through woodland. As you exit the woodland, ignore a footpath to your left and another at a bend in 200 yards and soon meet a junction of bridleways by a house. *(1 mile)*

④ Turn left here on a bridleway along a farm drive that passes between fields and continues through pretty woodland. Bear right at a junction of lanes by a cottage and soon pass a pretty pond. Continue between the grand buildings of **South Park Farm**, no ordinary farm this. Keep ahead and go through a gate. Ignore side paths now and continue along the track, which offers far-reaching views. Remain on the track when it

THE BELL INN AT OUTWOOD MAKES THE PERFECT HALFWAY STOP

narrows and soon, at a fork, bear right along the bridleway to pass between the ancient buildings of **Lower South Park Farm**. *(1¹/₂ miles)*

⑤ As you exit the gateway turn right along a farm drive and, when a junction of bridleways is met by the gates to **Lodge Farm**, turn left and pass through a gate to continue on a fenced bridleway. Press on through a second gate and turn left along a cart track. Now keep to this pleasant track as it makes its way beside fields, often to the accompaniment of skylarks high above. Finally the track ends at a T-junction where the way is right along a bridleway to soon meet a road. *(1¹/₂ miles)*

⑥ Turn right along the road to reach **Outwood Common** by the windmill. Bear right across a small area of grass before **Outwood Mill** and pass to the right of the mill, keeping a hedgerow to your right. Soon meet a road with a marker post opposite. By turning right along the road for 50 yards, you will meet the Bell public house, a source of good wholesome refreshment. *(³/₄ mile)*

*Built in 1665, this post-mill is said to be the oldest working mill in Britain. By 1790 it had competition from a larger smock-mill next to it but that later fell* *into disrepair and finally collapsed during a storm in 1960. The mill is in full working order and opens to the public during summer afternoons on Sundays and bank holidays.*

⑦ Return to the signpost and bear right over a small part of the common to reach a quiet lane. Here turn right along it to pass **The Windmill Garage**. Ignore a right fork and, when the lane ends by cottages, go ahead over a stile and continue across a field. At the far side, ignore a path to your left and press on along the right-hand side of the next field to meet a stile

A PEACEFUL CART TRACK ON THE ROUTE

between two oak trees ahead of you. (³/₄ mile)

⑧ Cross the stile and ignore a path to the left and one ahead. Our way is rightwards along the field edge. After crossing a brook in a line of trees, bear diagonally left across a field to reach a stile. Now maintain direction over two further fields to meet a road by **Outwood Swan Sanctuary**. Turn left along the road and soon, at a bend, go right on a bridleway along a cart track. (1 mile)

⑨ At the end of woodland the track meets a T-junction. Go left here along the bridleway and keep to this lovely path as it passes through mature woodland. Later it rises and passes an isolated house where you maintain direction along a drive. Pass between the buildings of **Cucksey's Farm** to rejoin the junction of tracks you met earlier. (1 mile)

⑩ Here press on ahead along the bridleway and, when this soon bends sharply left, go ahead and cross a stile. Maintain direction now along a field edge and, at the end of the field, cross a brook and a

stile. Continue ahead alongside the next field until you are opposite a knoll to your right. Go left over a stile and continue ahead along a field edge. When you enter a second field, turn right along its edge and now keep ahead until you pass between the farm buildings of **Coldharbour Farm** to reach a lane. (³/₄ mile)

⑪ Bear right along the lane that rises sharply to meet a directional post at a junction of tracks and turn left on the bridleway signed **GW**. Ignore a right fork and continue on this pleasantly level path. Later, on a right bend, ignore a footpath to your left and soon pass between banks to meet a junction of tracks. Go ahead up a stony bridleway to meet a T-junction where you turn left and by remaining on the bridleway you finally pass by a pond to meet a road. Turn right along the road and soon turn left up steps on a **GW** signed enclosed path. The path will bring you to **Castle Square** where you should now turn right and retrace your steps to the starting point. (1¹/₂ miles)

Date walk completed:

# CHELSHAM, THE VANGUARD WAY AND TATSFIELD

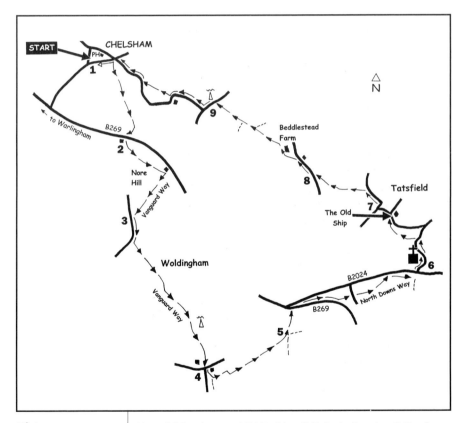

**Distance:**
10 miles

**Starting point:**
The village green at
Chelsham.
GR: 373590

Map: **OS Landranger 187 Dorking & Reigate Crawley & Horsham**

**How to get there:** *From the B269 at the southern end of
Warlingham, turn into Chelsham Road by Sainsbury's
supermarket and in 1/2 mile Chelsham village green will be
reached. Park alongside the green near the Bull Inn.*

THE OLD SHIP SITS IN A QUIET CORNER OF TATSFIELD, JUST A FEW YARDS FROM THE VILLAGE'S
PRETTY POND

*T*his outstanding circuit – best described as energetic – crosses the rolling downs that have made this area so well known to walkers. Following the Vanguard Way from Chelsham along a level track, it is not long before the path traverses appealing valleys, where the views are quite splendid. The route skirts the large houses of Woldingham, which cling to a steep hillside, before making its way to the top of the North Downs.

Here the path joins a splendid Neolithic trackway and continues along the ridge to later join the North Downs Way long distance path. A path over the open hillside offers views across the Weald that are outstanding. As the route begins to swing to the north, it passes Tatsfield's ancient church before meeting the Old Ship public house in a quiet corner of the village. More lovely field paths follow as the way continues through another pretty valley to rejoin the village green at Chelsham.

Tatsfield grew to its present size due to its closeness to the Biggin Hill aerodrome and many of its houses were described in the 1920s as little more than shacks. Well, times have changed and respectability has hit the village, which vies with Coldharbour and Hindhead to be Surrey's highest. Sitting near the pretty pond is the **Old Ship** public house, built in Victorian times. It makes a splendid place to stop: the comfortable bar and restaurant area is cosy, while the garden is splendid for summer use. The food ranges from filled baguettes to more substantial meals from the ever-changing menu on the blackboard. The beers on offer include Greene King IPA, Harvey's and Fuller's London Pride as well as the usual lagers, Guinness and Strongbow cider.

**Opening times** *are from 12 noon to 3 pm and 5.30 pm to 11 pm on Monday to Friday and from 11 am to 11 pm at weekends (10.30 pm Sunday). Cooked food is served from 12 noon to 2.30 pm and 7 pm to 9 pm (not on Sunday or Monday evenings), and booking is advisable. Telephone: 01959 577315.*

# The Walk

① The walk starts beside the **Bull Inn** on the centre of the village green. When facing the pub go right to a **Vanguard Way** sign on a short post and continue to soon meet a road. Turn left along the road and ignore two paths signposted on your right. At a road junction, turn right through a gate and continue on a bridleway along a track. Keep to the track as it follows the side of a field and when this ends, press on to meet a road. Turn right along the road to soon reach the B269. Now turn rightwards along it and in 80 yards turn left, following a path to the left of gated **Barnards Road**. *(1 mile)*

② After skirting a garden, the path passes through woodland to reach a stile in a field edge. Cross the stile and go half right over the crest of the field where you pass to the left of what looks like a bomb crater, soon followed by a dew pond. From here you should go slightly leftwards and aim for the right side of a house in the corner of the field by a marker post. Remaining on the **Vanguard Way**, you should turn right along the field edge, with a hedgerow to your left. With panoramic views across the valley, maintain direction down the hillside and at the bottom cross a farm track and continue along another field edge to finally meet a road. *(1 mile)*

*The 66-mile-long Vanguard Way path links Croydon to Newhaven*

119

*via Ashdown Forest. As silly as it may seem, the long distance path is named after a group of walkers who pioneered the route and once returned home in the guard's van of a crowded train.*

③ Turn left along the road and, when it bends to the right, bear left on a broad signposted bridleway. The bridleway now begins to climb and near the top of the incline it narrows and passes through woodland and continues along a farm track. Press on until after passing alongside the unusual wall

of **Flint House** you meet a road. *(1¹/₂ miles)*

④ Continue on the lane opposite and soon fork left by the entrance of a house on a path signposted as the **Vanguard Way**. Some 25 yards before reaching a stile ahead of you, leave the **Vanguard Way** by forking left on a narrower path. Ignore a stile in 50 yards and continue ahead to a second stile. Cross this and maintain direction alongside a wire fence. At the corner of this enclosure, ignore a stile ahead of you and turn right along the fence

JUST ONE OF THE SCENIC VALLEYS WHICH THIS UNDULATING ROUTE PASSES THROUGH

where, after going downhill for 70 yards, you meet and cross a stile to your left. Go ahead on a narrow path to meet a junction of tracks in 12 yards. Now fork left along a wide track that leads you through woodland. This Neolithic track eventually leads you to a gate by a wide crossing track. *(1 mile)*

⑤ Turn left here along the **North Downs Way** to reach a road junction. Here turn immediately right for 20 yards before going left and continuing along the **North Downs Way**. After remaining parallel to the road, it turns left up steps to meet a stile. Ignore a path to your left and continue ahead on the long distance path. Soon cross a quiet lane and press on through woodland to reach a field edge. Go ahead to a clump of trees and cross a stile; the path later brings you close to a road. Do not cross a stile to your left but continue along the **North Downs Way** until it finally leads you up steps to reach a road junction. *(1¹/₂ miles)*

⑥ Here leave the long distance path and continue up **Church Hill**, soon bearing left up more steps to enter the graveyard of **St Mary's church**.

*At almost 800 feet above sea level, St Mary's church is the highest in Surrey. Dating back to 1075 and built by the Normans, it has undergone restoration over the years, but the north wall and two lancet windows are the Norman originals. Inside there are old oak beams, a 500-year-old font and richly moulded original stonework. The flint tower is a much later addition from 1837.*

Pass to the right of the church to rejoin **Church Hill**. Turn left alongside the road and ignore a stile in a hedgerow to your left on a bend. When by the entrance to **Orchard Stables**, turn left up steps and continue on a fenced path. Keep to the path as it skirts fields and descends into a small valley. Cross a farm track and continue ahead over three small paddocks to reach a road. Turn left here and after 80 yards the **Old Ship** public house will be reached. *(³/₄ mile)*

⑦ After refreshment, cross the road and go ahead between cottages and the village pond to reach a children's playground. Bear right to meet a road and ignore a path on your right. Continue along the road, which soon leaves the houses behind and goes down a dip. As the road climbs out of the dip, go left and pass through a gate. Continue on a signed bridleway along the right side of a field. Press on alongside a second field that brings you into another valley and at the end of the field continue ahead on a well-worn path through trees. At the top of a rise, pass through a gate and maintain direction through the centre of a field to its top right corner where you will meet a lane. *(³/₄ mile)*

⑧ Turn right along the lane and when by the second house on your right, go left on a bridleway that crosses a corner of a field to meet a gate. Pass through the gate and go left for 10 yards before turning right on a track. Soon cross two stiles on your left to enter a field. Turn right along the field edge and cross another stile. Here take note of the landscape before you as the way heads directly towards a radio mast on the far side of the valley. Cross the two fields ahead of you and

press on ahead along a path. Later ignore a left turn and remain ahead to finally meet a road. *(1¹/₄ miles)*

⑨ Turn left along the road and at a road junction turn right and ignore footpath signs to left and right. Remain on the road until you meet a stile on your right at a sharp left bend by cottages. Go over the stile and cross the field diagonally leftwards to meet a stile hidden in trees in the top right corner. Maintain direction over the next field and cross a stile in the corner to the left of a bungalow. Now turn right along the road and at a junction turn left to meet the village green at **Chelsham** and the end of this super walk. *(1¹/₄ miles)*

Date walk completed:

# DORMANSLAND, MARSH GREEN AND DRY HILL

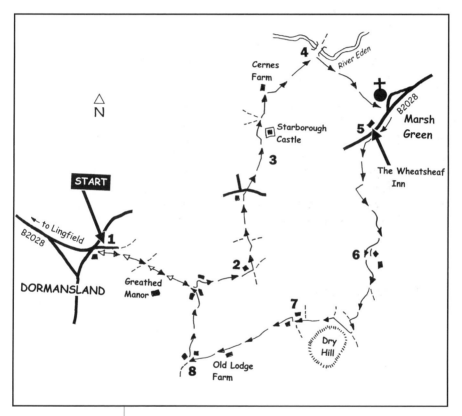

| Distance: | Map: OS Landranger 187 Dorking & Reigate, Crawley & Horsham |
|---|---|
| 8¹/₄ miles | |

**Starting point:**
Ford Manor Road,
Dormansland.
GR: 406427

**How to get there:** *Dormansland is 1 mile east of Lingfield on the B2028. From Lingfield travel east along the B2028, pass under a railway bridge and you will see Ford Manor Road at the second junction of roads on your right and to the left of the Plough Inn.*

THE WHEATSHEAF INN AT MARSH GREEN MAKES A GOOD PLACE TO STOP FOR REFRESHMENT

Starting from the magnificent parkland of Greathed Manor, the route goes over fields with wonderful views towards the North Downs. After skirting the grounds of Starborough Castle it meets the River Eden and crosses for a few yards into Kent where it reaches Marsh Green and the charming Wheatsheaf Inn.

From here, the way continues through still more scenic fields and begins a gentle climb on a drive where the views are breathtaking. Beyond Greybury Farm, an uphill track leads you through woodland and passes the indistinct remains of an Iron Age hill fort at Dry Hill. After following a private drive along the top of a ridge with outstanding views over the surrounding countryside, the route makes its way back to Dormansland. Please note that the grounds of Greathed Manor, through which this walk passes, are closed on 24th March each year.

This superb circuit is best left for the drier months, as it can get muddy during winter after prolonged rain.

124

The small community of Marsh Green and the **Wheatsheaf Inn** lie just a few yards over the border in Kent, but we can forgive the pub for that as it makes a very pleasant little place to stop for a bite to eat and to take on liquid refreshment. There is a garden for those who prefer to sit outdoors while recharging their batteries, and inside the pumps dispense Harvey's Best and Fuller's London Pride bitters plus six regularly changing guest ales. There are also Foster's, Stella Artois and Carling lagers plus Strongbow cider and Guinness – all in all a pretty wide choice. A good range of pub food is also available, served in ample proportions.

*Opening times are from 11 am to 11 pm (Sunday 12 noon to 10.30 pm). Cooked food is served from 12 noon to 2 pm and 7 pm to 9.30 pm (9 pm on Sunday). Booking for meals is necessary at weekends or if you are in a large group. Telephone: 01732 864091.*

# The Walk

① With your back to the B2028, walk along **Ford Manor Road** and, as it ends by a fork, continue along the right fork that is the driveway to **Greathed Manor**.

*Robert Kerr, the author of a then famous book,* **The Gentleman's House,** *designed Greathed Manor. Originally calling it Ford Manor, he built it in 1868 and seems to have enjoyed mixing Dutch, French, Italian and English styles together with no coherent bond. It is leased by the Country House Association and split into flats. A part of the house is open to the public from May to September on Wednesday and Thursday afternoons.*

Ignore a crossing path by a cottage and later pass the entranceway to the manor house. In 25 yards fork left through a gate to meet a barn. Turn left on a farm track to the left of the barn and follow it past farm buildings and a cottage. Now keep ahead on a bridleway that passes through woodland to reach a gate. Continue ahead along the bridleway as it goes between fields and comes to **Littleworth Cottage**. *(1¼ miles)*

② Some 50 yards after passing the cottage, ignore a bridleway to your right, but 50 yards later go left through a gate on a bridleway signed as the **Vanguard Way**. At a field keep ahead along the **Vanguard Way** to eventually meet a road by a row of cottages. Turn right along the road and in 30 yards go left over a stile and enter a large field. The way is diagonally right here to a stile in a line of trees. *(1 mile)*

③ Cross the stile and continue leftwards along a private drive to meet a junction of paths beside the entrance to **Starborough Castle**.

*Nothing now remains of the castle, once the home of Reginald, the first Lord Cobham, other than the remnants of a 14th century wall. On the inner side of the moat is the garden house of 1754*

*and stabling from the mid 18th century.*

Cross a stile on your left and turn right along the field edge to meet and cross a stile in the corner. Now turn right for 35 yards before crossing a stile on your left and continuing along another field edge. At the end of the field, go ahead along a farm track that runs along the left side of a small meadow. At the end of the meadow, and with **Cernes Farm** ahead of you, turn right along the meadow's edge and soon cross a stile in the corner. The

path forks here and our way is to go half left over a large field. Cross a stile and continue ahead on a track through a second field, and at a third field continue ahead to meet a bridge that crosses the **River Eden**. *(3/4 mile)*

④ Do not cross the bridge, but turn right along the riverbank to soon meet a farm track. Maintain direction now along this track and ignore another going off on your right. When the farm track turns sharply left, go ahead over a stile and cross a field in the direction of a church spire. At the far side cross a stile and continue on a path to reach the village green at **Marsh Green**. Turn right along the road to soon meet up with the **Wheatsheaf Inn**. *(3/4 mile)*

⑤ After taking on well-earned refreshment, continue alongside the road for a further 120 yards before turning left on a bridleway along **Greybury Lane**. Follow the quiet lane uphill where you are rewarded with breathtaking views over **Marsh Green** and beyond. As you near **Greybury Farm** and meet a fork in the drive, keep to the right-hand fork, signed as a bridleway, and skirt the gardens of a couple of impressive houses. *(1 1/2 miles)*

⑥ Keep ahead on the bridleway when the drive soon bends sharply left. The bridleway now goes

between fields to meet a track; continue ahead along this. Soon, at a fork, bear right along a sandy bridleway and ignore a couple of tracks to your right. Keep ahead when the path narrows and climbs more steeply to meet a T-junction by a marker post. Ignore the bridleway to the right, but turn leftwards on a signposted footpath to soon meet a junction of paths. Our route now goes right and continues uphill for a short distance on a well-trodden path. At a T-junction by a marker post, turn left and pass beside an orchard. *(3/4 mile)*

*Over to your left are the indistinct earthworks of the late Iron Age hill fort of Dry Hill. Covering 24 acres and about 1 mile in circumference, this is the largest hill fort in Surrey. The majority of people living in Surrey around 200 BC would have been farmers growing barley, oats and wheat, but in times of invasion or trouble they would withdraw into earthworks such as these for protection.*

⑦ Ignore a bridleway on your right as you approach a small group of cottages, but bear right along a bridleway after 100 yards at a junction of tracks. Press on along a tarmac drive where you are again treated to panoramic views over the surrounding countryside. The drive

LOOKING TOWARDS THE NORTH DOWNS

passes between well-maintained paddocks with very well cared for Arabian horses – no nags here as these are bred as pampered racehorses. Along the way, pass **Old Lodge Farm**, the centre of these equestrian activities. *(1 mile)*

⑧ When a barn and a house are met on your right, go right through a gate and pass between farm buildings. Now follow this signposted bridleway through a second gate and continue downhill through woodland. Keep ahead when you meet a drive and soon pass the side of stabling to reach a barn. Keep to the left of this and now continue along the drive of **Greathed Manor** to return to **Ford Manor Road** and the end of this excellent circuit. *(1¹/₄ miles)*

Date walk completed: